T0327256

— 2011 —

Editors
Sidney Gottlieb and Richard Allen

Editorial Advisory Board
Charles Barr   Thomas L. Leitch
James Naremore   David Sterritt
Michael Walker

Founding Editor
Christopher Brookhouse

Editorial Associate
Renata Jackson

Cover Design
Deborah Dutko

We evaluate manuscripts for the *Hitchcock Annual* throughout the year. Send correspondence and submissions to either Sidney Gottlieb, Department of Communications and Media Studies, Sacred Heart University, Fairfield, CT 06825 or Richard Allen, Department of Cinema Studies, New York University, Tisch School of the Arts, 721 Broadway, 6th floor, New York, NY 10003. E-mail addresses: spgottlieb@aol.com or Richard.Allen@nyu.edu

We invite articles on all aspects of Hitchcock's life, works, and influence, and encourage a variety of critical approaches, methods, and viewpoints. For all submissions, follow the guidelines of the *Chicago Manual of Style*, using full notes rather than works cited format. If submitting by mail, send two copies (only one of which will be returned) and return postage. But we prefer submissions via e-mail, which makes it easier to circulate essays for editorial review. The responsibility for securing any permissions required for publishing material in the essay rests with the author. Illustrations may be included, but as separate TIFF files rather than as part of the text file. Decision time is normally within three months. The submission of an essay indicates your commitment to publish it, if accepted, in the *Hitchcock Annual,* and that it is not simultaneously under consideration for publication elsewhere.

For all orders, including back issues, contact Columbia University Press, 61 West 62nd Street, New York, NY 10023; www.columbia/edu/cu/cup

The *Hitchcock Annual* is indexed in the *Film Literature Index* and *MLA International Bibliography.*

♔ Columbia University Press   *New York*

Columbia University Press
Publishers Since 1893
New York   Chichester, West Sussex

ISBN 978-0-231-16002-5 (pbk. : alk. paper)
ISSN 1062-5518

∞
Columbia University Press books are printed on
permanent and durable acid-free paper.
This book is printed on paper with recycled content.

Printed in the United States of America

p 10 9 8 7 6 5 4 3 2 1

HITCHCOCK ANNUAL
2011

Notorious: Hitchcock's Pivotal Film   *Thomas Leitch*   1

Family Dramas in Hitchcock's
Stage Fright   *Deborah Thomas*   43

"The Knock of Disapproval":
Juno and the Paycock and its
Irish Reception   *Charles Barr*   63

The Birds and the Kennedy Era   *John Hellmann*   95

Dial "M" for Museum:
The Hitchcock of Contemporary Art   *Erika Balsom*   129

"Murder Can Be Fun":
The Lost Music of *Frenzy*   *Gergely Hubai*   169

REVIEW ESSAY

Hitchcock Now   *James Naremore*   195

Contributors   207

THOMAS LEITCH

Notorious: *Hitchcock's Pivotal Film*

To claim that *Notorious* (1946) is the pivotal film in Alfred Hitchcock's career is not to claim that it is his greatest film, or even his first great film. From *The Lodger* (1926) to *Shadow of a Doubt* (1943), Hitchcock had made so many highly accomplished thrillers before *Notorious* that he was already widely regarded as the Master of Suspense. Nor did the film have any immediate effect on Hitchcock's reputation. Although it was a considerable box office success, it did not enjoy the same critical esteem as *The Lady Vanishes* (1938) or repeat the record of six Academy Award nominations, including Best Picture and Best Director (and one victory, for Miklós Rózsa's musical score), accorded *Spellbound* (1945), his immediately preceding film.[1] *Notorious* garnered nominations for only two Oscars, Claude Rains for Best Supporting Actor and Ben Hecht for Best Original Screenplay, and did not win either one. Nor did it win any awards when it was chosen for the 1946 Cannes Film Festival. *Notorious* did not mark a new era in Hitchcock's relationship with his collaborators or his studio. The package David O. Selznick sold to RKO so that he could concentrate on producing *Duel in the Sun* (King Vidor, 1946) included two stars who had already appeared in Hitchcock films, Cary Grant in *Suspicion* (1941) and Ingrid Bergman in *Spellbound*, which had also been scripted by Hecht. Hitchcock had never before worked with cinematographer Ted Tetzlaff or composer Roy Webb, and would never work with them again. Apart from that of Edith Head, the costume designer who was working with Hitchcock for the first of their ten collaborations, the most revealing credit in the film is notable for its absence. Because no one is credited as producer, film historians have agreed in assigning the role to Hitchcock himself, who became widely known as *de facto* producer on all his later films, even though he never took a producer credit.[2]

The pivotal status of *Notorious* is clear only in retrospect, within the context of Hitchcock's whole career. Although it is not strikingly original, it marks a turning point in Hitchcock's development. Before *Notorious,* Hitchcock had made many different kinds of films; after *Notorious,* he would with rare exceptions make only one kind, sticking not only to thrillers but to thrillers of a very particular sort. The film compounds several tendencies that had been gradually becoming more prominent in Hitchcock's work in a manner that is both definitive (no Hitchcock film is more fully achieved, with fewer false steps) and generative (its most distinctive concerns were subject to repeated reworking in his later films). *Notorious* reveals in an unprecedented way Hitchcock becoming what Charles Barr has called "the Hitchcock we all think we know."[3] Its importance is indicated by six tendencies whose combination proves distinctively and decisively Hitchcockian.

1. Psychological rather than physical violence. *Notorious* resolutely avoids violent imagery. Like the British industry in which he came of age, Hitchcock had never reveled in spectacular images of violence despite his close identification with the genre of the suspense thriller. *Blackmail* (1929), *Secret Agent* (1936), and *Foreign Correspondent* (1940) manage to stage their most violent scenes offscreen, often by cutting away from them abruptly. The death of Beaky Thwaite (Nigel Bruce) in France is only reported, never shown, in *Suspicion,* although Lina Aysgarth (Joan Fontaine) imagines it vividly. In *The Man Who Knew Too Much* (1934), the death of Louis Bernard (Pierre Fresnay) is so understated that even contemporary audiences have a hard time taking it seriously the first time they see it. Partly to appease industry censors, partly to display his own deadpan wit, Hitchcock excelled in implying violent death in charged moments more complex and powerful than staging these scenes directly.

Even so, Hitchcock's earlier films did not shy away from images of violent death. *Murder!* (1930), *Number Seventeen* (1932), and *Young and Innocent* (1937) all present scenes in which the initial discovery of a body is inflated by means of theatrical tableaux, juxtapositions of emphatic sights and sounds, or narrative consequences. Other films have more than their share of murder scenes, however elliptically these scenes may be presented. The opening shot of *The Lodger* presents a woman's silent scream as she dies. *The 39 Steps* (1935) shows the dying Annabella Smith (Lucie Mannheim) toppling onto the recumbent body of Richard Hannay (Robert Donat). *Sabotage* (1937) kills off all the people on a crowded bus. *The Lady Vanishes* cuts away from an image of the strangling of a musician to Miss Froy (Dame May Whitty) as she listens attentively to a tune that turns out to be the film's MacGuffin and then tosses the singer a coin, unaware that he has just been murdered. Hitchcock shows the stabbing of Aunt Patience (Marie Ney) in *Jamaica Inn* (1939), the fiery death of Ken Mason (Virgil Summers) in *Saboteur* (1942), the attempt by Charles Oakley (Joseph Cotten) to throw his niece Charlie (Teresa Wright) off a moving train and his own plunge to his death in *Shadow of a Doubt,* and the traumatic childhood death of his brother, impaled on a spiked fence, that haunts John Ballantine (Gregory Peck) throughout *Spellbound*.

Notorious, by contrast, seems to recoil from images of violence. T.R. Devlin (Cary Grant) dispassionately reports to Alicia Huberman (Ingrid Bergman) the suicide of her father (an uncredited Fred Nurney), imprisoned in Miami, as he and Alicia fly to Rio de Janeiro. The visceral impact of John Huberman's death by poison is further undercut by the fact that the audience's earlier acquaintance with him has been almost entirely auditory, based on the speech he makes to his daughter in the recorded conversation Devlin plays back for her and the abortive speech his lawyer cuts off in the courtroom in which he is sentenced to prison for treason. The audience's view of him in that scene is limited to a single

Figure 1

distant long take framed from within the rear doorway of the courtroom, a viewpoint from which Huberman's face can be seen only partially and momentarily (fig. 1). His voice both times we hear it seems as disembodied as the Voice of Terror in the 1942 Sherlock Holmes film of that title. After Eric Mathis (Ivan Triesault) announces his plan to toss his unreliable colleague Emil Hupka (Eberhardt Krumschmidt) from a moving car over a cliff on the way to Petropolis, the film fastidiously avoids showing the murder and never even indicates definitely that it happened. When Devlin asks Alicia how Hupka has acted since the party in which his nervous behavior alerted her to a suspicious wine bottle, she merely replies off-handedly, "Haven't seen him since."

By the end of the film, of course, it is Alicia herself whose life is in danger from the poison she has been slowly fed by Alex Sebastian (Claude Rains), the Nazi spy she has seduced and married at the behest of Paul Prescott (Louis Calhern) and her other handlers in the United States government, and his scheming mother (Leopoldine Konstantin). Hitchcock signals in several different scenes that Alicia is being poisoned. In the most famous of these, he frames her sitting with Alex, his

Figure 2

mother, and kindly Nazi physicist Dr. Anderson (Reinhold Schünzel), with an oversized cup of tea, reminiscent of the oversized glasses containing allegedly drugged drinks in *The Lady Vanishes*, looming in the foreground. While Alicia is listening to Dr. Anderson, who expresses concern about her health and inadvertently drops one last clue about his research into nuclear weaponry, he accidentally takes her teacup instead of her own, and the immediate and exaggerated concern expressed by the Sebastians alerts her to her own peril. As she struggles to rise from her chair in order to go upstairs and lie down, a brief but striking series of point-of-view shots show her view of first Alex and his mother, then their merging shadows, as figures nightmarishly distorted by the effects of the poison or her sudden paranoia (fig. 2). Alicia makes it only as far as the entrance hall before she collapses in a heap on the tiled floor.

This powerful moment certainly makes Alicia's physical distress palpable. But the emphasis, here and elsewhere, once the Sebastians have begun to poison her, is less on her physical than her psychological ordeal: her horrified realization that the husband she has been spying on knows

Figure 3

what she is doing, her sudden vertiginous isolation, her inability to save herself or reach out to her rescuer Devlin. Even when Devlin, disquieted by her failure to appear at their usual meeting place, appears at her house and insinuates himself into her bedroom, she seems to be in no pain because the Sebastians have given her "pills to make me sleep." The image that most suggests physical incapacity—the point-of-view shot of Alex and his mother, reduced to gaunt shadows, undulating spectrally before her eyes—suggests even more strongly Alicia's paranoia through its echo of the earlier series of point-of-view shots that showed Devlin askew (fig. 3) and then approaching Alicia, apparently gliding upside-down across her bedroom, as she unwillingly awoke from the bender during which they met to face the unwelcome hangover remedy Devlin pressed on her (fig. 4): a glass filled with a white liquid that glows as ominously as the glass of milk Lina Aysgarth suspects her husband Johnnie (Cary Grant) has poisoned in *Suspicion*. Both of the subjectively distorted sequences in *Notorious* use physical pain as a correlative for psychological strain, suggesting that the stress of drinking the wrong stuff has radically distorted Alicia's perceptions and

Figure 4

ultimately her sense of herself. This shift from physical to psychological violence is hardly surprising for a film Donald Spoto has called "Hitchcock's first attempt . . . [at] a serious love story."[4] Even more than *Rebecca* (1940) and *Shadow of a Doubt*, the film stylizes its violence by setting it in the context of what Marian Keane has called its "fairy tale" elements—the vulnerable princess, the sinister castle, the secret chamber, the climactic rescue from modern-day dragons—whose oneiric qualities both muffle the physical impact of violence and take precedence over it.[5] So the suicide of John Huberman, to take the obvious example, is less important for its physical violence than for its emotional impact on his daughter.

The films that follow *Notorious* are often equally intent on translating physical into psychological suffering. *The Paradine Case* (1947), which excludes violent scenes as rigorously as *Notorious*, concentrates instead on the psychological pressure the trial of Maddalena Paradine (Alida Valli) brings to bear on her barrister Anthony Keane (Gregory Peck); his wife Gay (Ann Todd); and Andre Latour (Louis Jourdan), the valet Keane seizes on as his principal suspect in the death of Colonel Paradine. *Under Capricorn* (1949), which shows no onscreen violence, devotes an unbroken nine-minute shot to the tormented confession of Lady Henrietta Flusky (Ingrid Bergman) that she killed her brother Dermot and allowed her groom and eloping lover Sam Flusky (Joseph Cotten) to take the blame for the crime. It is no coincidence that despite Hitchcock's repeatedly attested preference for strangulation as a murder method, both these films follow *Notorious* in focusing on cases of poisoning, a method whose apparent lack of cinematic possibilities he exploits just as carefully. *I Confess* (1952), *Rear Window* (1954), *To Catch a Thief* (1955), and *Family Plot* (1976) all minimize onscreen violence. *Topaz* (1969) so stylizes the death of Juanita de Cordoba (Karin Dor) that it becomes weirdly aestheticized. *The Trouble with Harry* (1955) uses the peregrinations of its inconvenient corpse as material for high comedy.

Hitchcock hardly eschews images of violence in his later films. *Rope* (1948) echoes *The Lodger* in its opening shot, which shows the murder of David Kentley (Douglas Dick), and *Rebecca* in its use of a moving camera to inscribe the absence of the victim during its voiceover narrative of his death, this time presented in the speculative voice of Rupert Cadell (James Stewart). The strangling sequence in *Dial M for Murder* (1953) ends with the spectacular 3-D impalement of the would-be murderer, C.A. Swann (Anthony Dawson), on a pair of scissors his intended victim, Margot Wendice (Grace Kelly), has plunged into his back. *The Man Who Knew Too Much* (1956) plays the murder of Louis Bernard (Daniel Gelin) much straighter than the corresponding shooting of Pierre Fresnay's character in the 1934 version, and in a more extended sequence whose murderous import is clear much earlier on. *Vertigo* (1958) apparently launches both characters played by Kim Novak from the bell tower of San Juan Bautista in two separate but equally harrowing scenes. Yet the impact of each of these sequences depends less on their visceral violence than on their emotional effects on the horrified survivors of each scene.

As the industry censorship that dictated the decorum of so many Hitchcock films began to relax, his presentations of violence become once again more extreme. The shower sequence in *Psycho* (1960), even though its only shot showing a knife touching flesh lasts less than a second, marks a turning point for the representation of violence in Hollywood. The attacks in *The Birds* (1963) are even more lengthy and graphic—though even these are photographed, like the murders in *Psycho*, with surprisingly little blood. The big set piece in *Torn Curtain* (1966) shows its hero Michael Armstrong (Paul Newman) killing Herman Gromek (Wolfgang Kieling), the bulldog police officer who has learned that Armstrong has only pretended to defect to East Germany and is really a double agent. And *Frenzy* (1972), the most physically uncompromising and disturbing of all Hitchcock's films, refuses to turn away from the unspeakably cruel rape and murder of Brenda Blaney (Barbara Leigh-Hunt). For all their often explicit representations of violence, however, Hitchcock's films after *Notorious* continue his project of undermining the assumption that the more graphic the violence, the more intimate the audience's emotional connection with its victims.

Even at its most shockingly explicit, Hitchcock's violence continues to serve essentially psychological ends. Once their early set pieces have unsettled the audience, *Psycho*, *The Birds*, and *Frenzy* deploy less and less violence as they go along. *Psycho* cuts away abruptly from the murder of Arbogast (Martin Balsam), and after the camera in *Frenzy* tracks out from what is about to become the murder scene of Barbara Milligan (Anna Massey) to create an effect more desolate than violent, the subsequent sequence showing her murderer, Bob Rusk (Barry Foster), attempting to find her corpse in a potato sack so that he can recover his initialed stickpin from her dead fingers is played as Grand Guignol comedy. *The Birds* does not show the birds' attack on the Brenner house but only the frightened reactions of the besieged inmates as they cower listening to the sounds of the assault. Even the film's climactic episode, which takes Melanie Daniels (Tippi Hedren) to the Brenner attic for another murderous attack, emphasizes the resulting psychological trauma over her physical suffering.

The place of *Notorious* in this sequence is clear. Hitchcock's early films present scenes of suffering that can move the audience to an emotional reaction by means of a pathetic and empathetic appeal. Beginning with *Notorious*, he shifts to using physical violence as a figure for psychological violence, whether that of the characters or the audience. This psychological violence rather than the physical violence that figures it becomes the focus of Hitchcock's later films. Armstrong's killing of Gromek in *Torn Curtain* emphasizes not the suffering of the victim but, more surprisingly, the strain on his killer, who tries one way after the other to kill him silently, only to discover how agonizingly difficult it is to take the life of a man who does not want to die. No wonder that Robin Wood observed as long ago as 1965 that many commentators on *The Birds*, the most spectacular and unpsychological film Hitchcock ever made, contend that the birds' attacks *"express the tensions between the characters"*—a tendency that has only become more pronounced in the half-century since Wood wrote.[6] For ever since *Notorious*, Hitchcock had been using violence primarily as a means of imaging and exploring psychological trauma.

2. Dramatic irony instead of mystery. A staple of Hitchcock interviews is his dislike of the whodunit, which sacrifices two hours of suspense for ten seconds of surprise when the killer is revealed in the climactic scene. But in fact many of Hitchcock's own thrillers incorporate whodunit elements. Broadly speaking, these elements predominate in Hitchcock's stories of domestic crime and recede in his tales of espionage. Virtually all of Hitchcock's domestic crime dramas require detective figures to identify a killer in order to vindicate an innocent suspect, a formula that is complicated by the surprising climactic revelation in *Stage Fright* (1950). *Murder!* and *Young and Innocent* are formally whodunits, searches by amateur detectives for amateur murderers. *The Lodger* is a did-he-do-it best described by the title of the 1916 play by Marie Belloc Lowndes and H.A. Vachell on which it is largely based—*Who Is He?*—a title that would have been equally appropriate for *Suspicion, Shadow of a Doubt,* and

Spellbound. (*Who Is She?* would have been an apt title for *The Paradine Case* and *Under Capricorn*, and *Who Was She?* for *Rebecca*.) *The Lady Vanishes* asks both what happened to Miss Froy and who was responsible. Even *The Farmer's Wife* (1928) could be described as a romantic variation of a whodunit whose leading question is not "Who killed Farmer Sweetland's wife?," whom we see dying of natural causes in the opening scene, but rather "Who will take her place?"

Whodunits, as Hitchcock observed, depend on mystifying the audience by withholding important information from them until the end of the film. But even thrillers that are not whodunits, such as *Under Capricorn, Vertigo, Psycho,* and *Marnie* (1964), often depend for their success on the formula of mystification and climactic surprise that Hitchcock disavowed. His own stated preference was for the opposite technique, dramatic irony. As he told an interviewer in 1966, "Suspense can only be achieved by telling the audience as much as you can"—more, in fact, than the characters know.[7]

The most common occasion for dramatic irony in Hitchcock's early films is romantic triangles. With very rare exceptions like Noel Coward's 1932 play *Design for Living* and the 1933 Ernst Lubitsch film based on it, such triangles depend on two lovers keeping their liaison a secret from a third party, but not from the audience. (Hitchcock's own romantic comedy, *Mr. and Mrs. Smith* [1941], would fit this unusual everyone-knows-everything pattern if only Ann Krausheimer Smith [Carole Lombard] and Jeff Custer [Gene Raymond] were really lovers.) The audience knows more than at least one member of the triangle for much of the running time of *The Ring* (1927), *The Manxman* (1929), *Blackmail, Rich and Strange* (1932), and *Waltzes from Vienna* (1933). In every case, the audience's superior knowledge intensifies both their curiosity about what will happen next and their rooting interest in the romantic relationships involved.

Apart from these romantic triangles, Hitchcock's early films tend to restrict their audience's point of view largely to that of a single figure or couple who knows as much as the audience. Their lack of foreknowledge means that the audience experiences the bumpy adventures of Roddy Berwick in *Downhill* (1927), the Lawrence family in *The Man Who Knew Too Much* (1934), Richard Hannay in *The 39 Steps*, and Richard Ashenden (John Gielgud) and Elsa Carrington (Madeleine Carroll) in *Secret Agent* as a series of shocks and surprises, very much as the heroes and heroines themselves do. The most celebrated example of dramatic irony in Hitchcock's early thrillers—the 240-foot crane shot across the crowded ballroom of the Ritz Hotel to an extreme close-up of the twitching eyes that identify the band's drummer (George Curzon) as the murderer of Christine Clay (Pamela Carme) in *Young and Innocent*—instantly turns the film's search for the solution to the mystery into an exercise in dramatic irony, as Erica (Nova Pilbeam) despairs of identifying the murderer the audience knows is sitting on a prominently raised platform only two rooms away from her. But this extraordinary moment, which changes both the direction and the mood of the film, comes only a few minutes before it ends, as a prevision of the climactic discovery Erica is about to make herself.

As early as *Rich and Strange* and *Sabotage,* Hitchcock experiments with more extended dramatic ironies as devices that can structure his films by organizing the audience's responses to them. But dramatic irony did not begin to dominate his films until he came to America. In *Foreign Correspondent,* the audience learns before Huntley Haverstock, *né* Johnny Jones (Joel McCrea), does that peace activist Stephen Fisher (Herbert Marshall) is actually a German spy and that Rowley (Edmund Gwenn), the bodyguard he has arranged to protect Haverstock, has actually been assigned to kill him. Hitchcock presents Uncle Charlie in an equivocal light in the opening sequence of *Shadow of a Doubt,* long before his niece has reason to suspect his sinister background, and then makes the audience wait for young Charlie's awareness to catch up with their own. He reveals the treachery of Willie (Walter Slezak), the U-boat captain whom the survivors of *Lifeboat* (1944) have rescued, to the audience before first Gus Smith (William Bendix) and then the others realize he is steering their boat into the path of a

German warship. In *Rebecca, Saboteur, Spellbound,* and even *Suspicion,* however, Hitchcock refuses to reveal any more to the audience than to the second Mrs. de Winter (Joan Fontaine), Barry Kane (Robert Cummings), Dr. Constance Petersen (Ingrid Bergman), or Lina Aysgarth, forcing us to experience their stories by following the same clues they do.

Notorious sets the path for Hitchcock's later films by wedding the dramatic irony he had heretofore generally reserved for romantic triangles to the suspense of the thriller. It is not surprising that except for *Mr. and Mrs. Smith,* the film features the most prominent romantic triangle in Hitchcock since *Waltzes from Vienna* (1933), for such triangles and the kind of suspense they generated had no place in the world of the British thrillers that made Hitchcock famous. The exception that proves the rule is Iris Henderson's engagement to the "blue-blooded check-chaser" Charles Fotheringale, who is appropriately kept offscreen until he is glimpsed briefly at Victoria Station after she has been safely paired with the more appropriate romantic partner Gilbert, who is never called on to compete with her fiancé. Men on the run have to settle for romance on the run, and amateur sleuths like Gilbert and Erica Burgoyne are too focused on the questions of whodunit and what will happen next to become romantically involved with more than the single, available partner whose love is their commission.

Notorious is the first Hitchcock film to make its romantic triangle the basis of its suspense. The film contains virtually no mystery of the sort that had animated his British thrillers. The audience knows from the beginning that Alicia is a woman of questionable virtue, the daughter of a traitor, and once we learn of her assignment to infiltrate Alex Sebastian's household, there is no doubt that Sebastian and his colleagues are up to no good. When she falls ill, the audience knows she is being poisoned, and we know who the poisoners are. The film's only formal mystery—why was Emil Hupka so troubled by the sight of one of the wine bottles displayed on a sideboard in Sebastian's house?—is resolved shortly after it is posed, and very incompletely resolved as well. Presumably Hupka feared that the bottle he saw contained the uranium ore that had been secreted in other bottles in Sebastian's wine cellar. But it is never explained why Sebastian chose wine bottles as his hiding place or why Hupka came to mistake one bottle for another, because Hitchcock is not really interested in the mystery; rather, he is using the wine bottles only as a MacGuffin to express, explore, and intensify the romantic intrigue among his three leading characters.

What *Notorious* lacks in mystery it makes up in dramatic irony. The audience knows before Alicia does (although she certainly suspects it after he prevents her from getting a speeding ticket) that Devlin is some kind of government agent. Long before she does, we know that even though he refuses to say so, Devlin loves her. Even if we missed the telling glance he gives her as she looks out the airplane window to see Rio de Janeiro spread out before her, we would certainly know his feelings from his acid defense of her to Prescott's colleague, intelligence agent Walter Beardsley (Moroni Olsen), when her assignment to seduce Sebastian is revealed to him, along with her alleged fitness for it: "Miss Huberman is first, last, and always not a lady. She may be risking her life, but when it comes to being a lady, she doesn't hold a candle to your wife, sir, sitting in Washington playing bridge with three other ladies of great honor and virtue." Devlin's failure to express his admiration and love to Alicia herself, his "refus[al] to pronounce the saving 'word,'" creates the "misunderstanding" Eric Rohmer and Claude Chabrol see as "the key to all Hitchcock's films."[8]

As the film proceeds, the audience develops a stronger and stronger rooting interest in the keepers of its various secrets precisely because they are keeping secrets we urgently wish to be preserved or revealed. We know before Sebastian does that Alicia has married him only in order to spy on him, and we know before Alicia does that Sebastian is on to her. Hitchcock's suspense depends on our wanting Alicia's secret to remain a secret from him and on our wanting Sebastian's secret to become known to her. The suspense is intensified by a brilliant twist. Instead of allowing Sebastian to confront Alicia in the wine cellar with the fact that he has learned the truth about her, the film withholds his full discovery of her

Figure 5

perfidy until later and then shares his discovery with his mother rather than her. The result is that not only has Sebastian realized that Alicia is an American agent, but Alicia "is totally unaware of what Alex has learned."[9]

During Alicia and Devlin's last rendezvous on the park bench, we know, as Devlin does not, that she is sick, and we know, as Alicia does not, that her sickness is caused by poison. Many members of the audience find their knowledge here such a burden that they want to shout to Devlin, "How can you let her leave? Do you really think she's been drinking again? Don't you see that she's been poisoned?"[10] When Devlin changes his mind about Alicia's condition—"She wasn't drunk. She was sick"—the audience is happy to accept his apparently arbitrary change of diagnosis because we are so eager for him to rescue Alicia. Even as Devlin, appearing at Sebastian's house and finally attesting his love for Alicia, walks her down the interminable staircase to the front door (fig. 5), we still know a vital secret Sebastian is desperate to keep from his Nazi colleagues: that he has been poisoning his wife not only because she is an American spy but because Hupka's fate has made him see that his own life depends on keeping her betrayal from them. And we are equally desperate that this secret remain a secret for as long as it takes Devlin and Alicia to escape the house, at the exact moment that the conspirators realize they have been duped. It is only when all the characters come into possession of all the truth that the film can come to an end.

Once Hitchcock had discovered the power of dramatic irony to shape the Hitchcock thriller, he never looked back. Even subsequent films that incorporate elements of mystery, from *Stage Fright* and *To Catch a Thief* to *Vertigo, Marnie,* and *Frenzy,* are dominated by the dramatic irony that favors suspense over surprise. As Todd McGowan has observed, the fatal stabbing of Marion Crane (Janet Leigh) in *Psycho* is not only the most celebrated surprise in the history of cinema but a setup for all the suspense that follows once we know, or think we know, that Mrs. Bates has killed Marion—most notably, in the stabbing of the private detective Arbogast (Martin Balsam), "an experience of suspense that depends on the earlier surprise."[11] The flashback that accompanies the letter Judy Barton (Kim Novak) begins to write Scottie Ferguson (James Stewart) confessing her complicity in the scheme of Gavin Elster (Tom Helmore) to murder his wife instantly turns the film's central mystery—why has Madeleine Elster (Novak) been acting so strangely?—into an exercise in dramatic irony. More often, such exercises are at the center of Hitchcock's later films, as they are in *Rope, Strangers on a Train* (1951), *I Confess, Dial M for Murder,* and *North by Northwest* (1959). Our experience of all these films is defined by the secrets they reveal to us early on: that Brandon (John Dall) and Philip (Farley Granger) have staged their dinner party as a celebration for their murder of David Kentley; that Bruno Anthony (Robert Walker), not Guy Haines (Granger), murdered Guy's wife Miriam (Laura Elliott); that Father Michael Logan (Montgomery Clift) cannot speak out to exonerate himself of murder because the real murderer, Otto Keller (O.E. Hasse), revealed his guilt under the seal of confession; that Tony Wendice (Ray Milland) is plotting first to have his wife killed, and then, when that plan falls through, to get her convicted of murder; and that Roger Thornhill (Cary Grant) will never be able to persuade Philip Vandamm (James Mason), the "importer-exporter" of "government secrets" who has mistaken him for federal agent George Kaplan, that he is mistaken because George Kaplan does not exist.

3. A tone at once more complex and more unified. The tone of *Notorious,* consistently witty but rarely funny, was the product of Hitchcock's long years of experimentation with the relationship between melodrama and humor. Even before he made the thriller his stock-in-trade, he had delighted in mixing moments of incongruous absurdity or farce into his melodramas, from the dog that licks the bare foot of Jill Cheyne (Carmelita Geraghty) as she kneels in prayer in *The Pleasure Garden* (1925) to Rasi's rescue *en deshabille* from a burning building in *Waltzes from Vienna.* These often disorienting shifts from "grave to gay" became Hitchcock's trademark even before his identification with the thriller.[12] Hitchcock's early non-thrillers are typically marked by a thoroughgoing alternation of melodrama and farce. *The Ring* sets its romantic triangle amid the comic types of a traveling sideshow. *Rich and Strange* begins its *Candide*-ish saga of innocents abroad as escapist fantasy and ends in shipwreck without ever abandoning its oscillation between the high-toned declamations of office drudge Fred Hill (Henry Kendall) and the comic misadventures that continually deflate them. Even *Juno and the Paycock* (1930), which Hitchcock disavowed as a film that followed Sean O'Casey's play so closely that "it had nothing to do with cinema," is structured by its grim puncturing of stock Irish characters' comically inflated pretensions.[13]

Small wonder, then, that Hitchcock's earliest thrillers regularly leaven their melodrama with moments of gaiety, even if those moments have a darker payoff. Crewe (Cyril Ritchard), the artist who takes Alice White (Anny Ondra) home to his studio, forces himself on her after encouraging her to paint a risqué picture, dressing her as a ballerina, and singing a song identifying her with "Miss Up-to-Date." Killing the artist turns every detail of Alice's mundane life that night and the following day into an ironic reminder of her nightmarish misadventure. The contrast is most economically encapsulated in the image of Alice's accuser, a painting of a laughing court jester pointing out into the space of first the artist's studio and then the police station where Alice's confession is cut short by the arrival of Frank, who takes her off to a deeply uncertain future. Five years later, the real threats to European peace in general and the Lawrence family in particular in *The Man Who Knew Too Much* (1934) are at once defused and intensified by a comic undercurrent that encourages viewers to let down their guard over and over so that they can be frightened again and again.

Once Hitchcock had refined this formula by telegraphing most of the important shifts in tone in *The 39 Steps,* he could readily become identified with the seriocomic thriller he had virtually invented. If it had been up to Hitchcock, his American films might well have continued this series without a break. The preliminary treatment for *Rebecca* he drafted along with Joan Harrison and Philip MacDonald began with a boldly farcical sequence on the Riviera in which Max de Winter, taking a speedboat to join his friends aboard a yacht, blows cigar smoke into the face of his future bride, making her throw up overboard.[14] Selznick, who vetoed the scene in no uncertain terms, demanded an adaptation that stuck closer to Daphne du Maurier's best-selling novel, and Hitchcock's Oscar-winning film did just that, reserving its comedy for marginal elements, especially Florence Bates's performance as the vulgar, pushy Edythe Van Hopper, that receded as the story gathered momentum. Yet the scene in which Max's bride begins by laughing at movies he has made on their honeymoon and ends with her despairing offer to leave their marriage shows how committed Hitchcock remained to leavening his melodrama with humor.

Largely in response to Selznick's strictures, Hitchcock developed a new tone whose humor was more subdued and more tightly integrated into the prevailing melodrama. The director, whose fondness for Thomas De Quincey's essay "On Murder, Considered as One of the Fine Arts" was well-known, might well have drawn inspiration from an earlier De Quincey essay, "On the Knocking at the Gate in *Macbeth*" (1823), which asks why the porter's drunken knocking after the murder of Duncan "reflect[s] back upon the murderer a peculiar awfulness and depth of solemnity." After observing that a murderer like Macbeth is animated by "some great storm of passion,—jealousy, ambition, passion, hatred,— which will create a hell within him," De Quincey concludes that "in order for a new world ["the world of devils"] to step in, this world must for a time disappear." The knocking of the drunken porter at the gate marks "the return of ordinary life": "the re-establishment of the goings-on of the world in which we live first makes us profoundly sensible of the awful parenthesis that had suspended them."[15] Increasingly as Hitchcock's career develops, his shifts in tone express not merely an alternation between grave and gay but an emphasis on melodrama as uncanny and surreal by contrasting moments of emotional intensity with the rhythms of everyday life.

Throughout *Notorious*, Hitchcock's wit intensifies both the nightmare quality of Alicia's ordeal and its emotional seriousness. The film's only moments of outright comedy all come in the very beginning. As he and Alicia leave her own drunken party to go for a drive, Devlin parks her empty glass between the breasts of a guest who has passed out on her sofa. Once they are outside, he produces a bandanna that he decorously ties around her exposed midriff, supposedly to prevent her from catching a cold. Settled behind the wheel and driving at a reckless speed, she complains that the fog makes it hard to see. A point-of-view shot indicates that the occlusion is actually her untended hair, which is blowing over her face.

Not only does the film not continue to joke; it uses every one of these opening jokes to set up more serious concerns about Alicia's alcoholism, the extent to which she can count on Devlin to take care of her, and the ways in which drinking alters her perception and makes her more vulnerable to predatory men, from the motorcycle cop who will shortly pull her over to the emotionally remote government agent who will prostitute her to the husband who will poison her.

As the film continues, it settles into a groove marked not by an oscillation between comedy and melodrama but by a single tone, witty and amusing but not funny, consistently characterized by dramatic irony. When Devlin, to whom Alicia has just passed the key to her husband's wine cellar during a formal party, has indicated the possibility that the champagne will run out and send Sebastian to the wine cellar himself, the very next shot presents perhaps the wittiest of all Hitchcock's cameos, as the director downs a glass of champagne to deplete the supply. After Devlin has discovered the secret of the wine cellar by accidentally breaking a bottle there and discovering that it is full of "some kind of metal ore," Alicia says, "I'm terrified," and he replies, "Pretend you're a janitor. Janitors are never terrified." His jest lightens the mood of the scene while reminding the audience that Alicia is not a janitor but a bride threatened with discovery by the husband she is betraying.

This relentlessly witty, insinuating use of dramatic irony was not original with *Notorious,* or indeed with Hitchcock. Ernst Lubitsch had employed a naughtier version of it for years in his comedies. Hitchcock's distinctive contribution was to use dramatic irony to lighten and paradoxically to unify the tone of his thrillers even as it multiplied the stakes by intensifying the audience's investment in the story and their rooting interest in the characters. Shorn of the incidental touches of comic relief in *The 39 Steps, The Lady Vanishes, Foreign Correspondent,* and *Shadow of a Doubt,* this witty use of dramatic irony made those touches seem extraneous.

Perhaps the master key to this shift in Hitchcock's tone is Cary Grant's performance as Devlin. Grant, a favorite of Hitchcock's because of his mastery of both grave and gay registers, here gives what Susan White calls "his usual lightness . . . a leaden core."[16] Peter Bogdanovich has described Devlin as "unquestionably the darkest characterization of

Cary Grant's career."[17] Why does he come across as even darker than Johnnie Aysgarth, whose wife worries that he is planning to kill her in *Suspicion*? Because whether or not Lina's suspicions are accurate, she is surely correct in describing Johnnie as a child with all a child's charm, impulsiveness, and appetite for play—an appetite that is brought out most fully in his scenes with Beaky Thwaite, the old friend Lina eventually comes to believe Johnnie has murdered. The puzzle of *Suspicion* is how to reconcile Johnnie's foolishly childish appetites with his calculating means of satisfying them. In place of such a blank contradiction, *Notorious* offers a blank slate. Devlin smiles constantly but never laughs or makes Alicia laugh. He never confesses his love for her until the final sequence, though Hitchcock's tautly controlled dramatic irony makes it plain to everyone in the audience. Devlin is as charming, polished, and handsome as Johnnie, but as obscure to the heroine as the brooding heroes of Gothic romances. The impenetrability of his façade makes his blandly clipped charm more menacing than Johnnie's impetuous appetites, even if they included murder, could ever be.

4. Watching without watching. It is a commonplace of the critical discourse on spy films that they assign central importance to the act of watching. What is more seldom observed is that successful spies, in fiction as in real life, are those who can watch without seeming to watch. The representation of spies constitutes a special problem for cinema, which must constantly find interesting and expressive ways to mask the professional gazes they present. *Notorious* tackles this problem by presenting each moment of looking-without-seeming-to-look in terms of what Sidney Gottlieb has called "the averted gaze," cloaked in the facial and gestural language of sexual flirtation.[18] The film is a virtual anatomy of averted gazes organized under a series of overlapping categories that link spying to romance, beginning with a category common to all espionage films and then proceeding through a series of categories that indicate more and more clearly its links to both romance and psychopathology.

Looking while pretending that you're not looking. This trope of espionage is modeled by the first spy the film presents, the agent walking along the street past Alicia's Miami bungalow without looking at it directly. (Alicia's later reference to "that buzzard with the glasses" indicates that he has not succeeded in avoiding her notice.) When Alicia first arrives at Sebastian's house, a series of tracking shots suggest that she is trying her best to take in her surroundings without seeming to pry. Later in this sequence, she does everything she can to hide the fact that she is alertly watching her surroundings, the other guests, and especially Hupka's agitation over the wine bottle. Alicia's success in getting Sebastian to hand over the household keys in his mother's charge and the subsequent montage of closet doors opening to her gaze demonstrate a triumph of watching that does not look to her unsuspecting bridegroom like watching.

Looking furtively because you're aware that you're being watched. In the following scene at the racetrack, Alicia and Devlin, aware that Sebastian may be watching them, avoid making eye contact, even as they hurl recriminations at each other, during what they hope to pass off as a chance meeting. During the party sequence, neither Alicia nor Devlin ever looks at the key to the wine cellar, even though it is the only reason Alicia has arranged the party. Although they frequently look directly at each other before going down to the wine cellar, their *sotto voce* dialogue reveals that their smiles and laughter are all assumed for the sake of Sebastian, who is keeping a close eye on them. Later, when Sebastian discovers them in the wine cellar, Devlin pulls Alicia into a tight embrace in order to fool Sebastian into mistaking their professional collaboration for a romantic liaison. The moment takes off from the opposition between espionage and romance that had run throughout *Secret Agent.* But it is far more ironic and complex, because here the romance that is supposed to mask spying is in fact the motive for the spying: Devlin is forcing Alicia to act out the emotions she really feels for him, and to act them out for a hostile audience she must convince. Their refusal to meet each others' eyes goes far beyond

Figure 6   Figure 7

performing for an audience, as they show when they are alone on the park bench where they meet in Rio or in the car that takes them to the riding club.

Expressing power by withholding the gaze. Hitchcock first introduces Devlin by a medium shot of the back of his head as he sits in Alicia's party. He is clearly watching her, but we never see him watching; the gaze he directs at her is withheld from us. Much later, Madame Sebastian routinely expresses her power by focusing on her embroidery instead of watching Sebastian as he tells her of his wedding plans or Alicia as she is poisoning her or sitting at her bedside waiting for her to die.

Looking away because you're staking yourself out to be looked at. When Devlin takes Alicia to a riding club, he expects Sebastian to recognize her as an old friend. As Devlin and Alicia ride past Sebastian and a female companion, Alicia does indeed recognize Sebastian, but he fails to recognize her because her hat is pulled low over her eyes, and she is trying not to look as if she is looking at him even as she struggles to catch his attention. Interestingly, the shot from Alicia's point of view shows Devlin riding between her and Sebastian, while Sebastian's matching point-of-view shot omits Devlin and shows the unrecognized Alicia alone (figs. 6 and 7).

Accepting yourself as someone who doesn't have the power to look back. The film's first sequence ends with Alicia emerging from the courtroom where her father has just been convicted of treason, first looking down, then looking past the reporters and press photographers gathered outside to question and photograph her. Throughout the film thereafter, Alicia

Figure 8   Figure 9

repeatedly fails to meet the gaze of intimidating characters. She cannot meet Devlin's steady gaze the morning after she first meets him, or the Commodore's questioning gaze when he appears at the end of the scene to renew his invitation for a cruise. She repeatedly wilts before the gazes of both Alex and his mother. In her first scene with Alex, she repeatedly fails to meet his eyes, and she ends the scene by casting her eyes downward as he wonders, "What shall we have for our first dinner together?" Her opposite number in this regard is Madame Sebastian, who first introduces herself to Alicia and the audience by advancing toward the camera with a boldly appraising gaze (fig. 8) and subsequently coolly watches Sebastian as he scans the crowd at the racetrack through a pair of binoculars (fig. 9). Later, Sebastian himself cannot meet his mother's gaze as he confesses that "I am married to an American agent."

Disavowing the gaze. Sebastian is not the only person who encounters Alicia and Devlin in the wine cellar. Close behind him is his servant Joseph (Alex Minotis). Joseph sees everything Sebastian sees, but he looks away hastily because he does not want to see what he is seeing. Unwilling to take responsibility for his gaze, he discreetly disavows it. A more sinister version of this disavowal had already been presented at the end of Alicia's first dinner in Sebastian's house, when Sebastian refused to meet the eyes of the hapless Hupka, or indeed of any of his other conspirators in the scene, as Mathis led him off to his death (fig. 10). Later, neither Sebastian nor his mother looks directly at Alicia as he urges her to drink the first cup of coffee he has poisoned.

Figure 10

Looking insecure. Unlike James Bond and other spies whose stock-in-trade is personal charisma, Hitchcock's amateur spies are always insecure, none more than Alicia. At the track, she watches a race through a pair of binoculars in order to motivate her inability to look Devlin in the face as he condemns her for the sexual licentiousness that allowed her to succeed at the job he gave her. Eventually, however, she is so overcome with emotion that she lowers the binoculars in the middle of the race and casts her eyes downward in distress. It is her signature look in the film, one she repeats at the end of the following scene, when the American agents agree that it would be "the cream of the jest" if she married Sebastian, and Devlin leaves the room as she surrenders to despair.

Although the insecurity and powerlessness indicated by the averted gaze is often construed as conventionally feminine, both inside and outside of movies, Devlin, who avoids looking directly at Alicia for most of this scene, is equally capable of revealing his insecurity through averted gazes, even when no one is watching him.[19] When Joseph tells him that Alicia is seriously ill, he looks abruptly away from him. Throughout the film, he conceals his insecurity from

Figure 11

Alicia even as he reveals it to the audience by the furtive way he watches her. As Alicia drunkenly accelerates from forty to eighty miles an hour, he pretends not to be paying attention even as he reaches a wary hand out to the steering wheel (fig. 11). Although he and Alicia look directly at each other throughout their first scene at an outdoor cafe in Rio de Janeiro—the only such scene in the film—he repeatedly looks away from her as she taunts him for his fear of her in the following scene, right up until the moment of their first kiss.

When Alicia is preparing for her dinner at Sebastian's house, Devlin studiously peruses a magazine, his gaze downcast, as Prescott fastens the rented jewels around her neck. He greets the news that Sebastian has asked Alicia to marry him with only a hooded glance from the corner of his eye (fig. 12). Even during the most romantic sequence of the film, the unbroken two-and-a-half-minute take showing the couple kissing just before Devlin leaves to get Alicia's assignment, he rarely meets her eyes. Instead he is shown in profile, his eyelids lowered, in a more discreet and less revealing version of Alicia's downcast gaze. Although Devlin is shown at both the racetrack and

Figure 12

Figure 13

Sebastian's house obviously looking for Alicia, he repeatedly looks away from her once he has found her. The single shot in which he watches her most frankly and attentively is the moment when he has first brought her together with Sebastian (fig. 13).

Early on in the film, Alicia suggests to Devlin, who is by training and profession a spy, that he keeps women at a distance because "you're scared of yourself." He brushes off her remarks, but from that point on, it is impossible to watch him watching her without seeing the gaze by which he keeps her at a distance as a sign of both sexual appetite and sexual insecurity, a vulnerability that constantly expresses itself to the audience, though rarely hereafter to Alicia, as a fear of emotional commitment. Sebastian's own gaze is even more explicitly marked by his lack of confidence. All the moments when he watches Alicia most vigilantly—at the racetrack, at the party, in the wine cellar, as she is sleeping afterwards, as she drinks the coffee he has poisoned—are the moments when he is most suspicious of her. Sebastian watches his bride precisely because he suspects her *bona fides*, and once his suspicions are confirmed, the film provides no further shots of him watching her.

Notorious loses interest in Sebastian's gaze once his feelings about Alicia have resolved into hatred. But Hitchcock's interest in baleful gazes remains just as lively. It is merely their direction and agency that have changed. Sebastian's fear that Alicia's identity as an American agent may compromise him despite her illness and death turns him in the film's final sequence from someone who watches to someone who is watched. Sebastian is far less intent on Alicia—his ministrations to the wife whose lover is taking her to the hospital are transparently unfeeling and ineffectual— than on the colleagues who are watching him for the same sorts of signs that betrayed Emil Hupka. In revenge for his pitiless surveillance of his wife, he is now subject to murderous scrutiny himself.

Not looking because you don't need to look, or because your look wouldn't communicate anything new. It is ironic that the film focuses so intently on the insecure gazes of Devlin and Sebastian and the coolly professional gazes of Madame Sebastian and the Nazis under which Sebastian is playing out the role of the devoted husband concerned for his ailing wife. For although she tells Devlin, "I don't go for patriotism, or patriots," and assures Sebastian, "I'm allergic to American agents," the most important spy is Alicia, the film's leading and most sympathetic character. Indeed, Richard Allen has singled out as "a tour de force of plot construction" the film's combination of "the joint quest narrative with *both* kinds of gendered-plot structure: the narrative of the male investigation of a woman (Devlin and Alicia) *and* the narrative of the 'gothic melodrama' involving the woman's investigation of a persecuting older man (Alicia and Alex)."[20]

Tania Modleski has noted that the film's heroine is "cast in the active role of knowledge-seeker: in her capacity as spy she becomes an investigator."[21] In the early scenes in which Alicia and Devlin size each other up, as John Orr points out, "the primal gaze is *hers*."[22] Yet Alicia, like Devlin, steadfastly avoids meeting the gaze of most of the men who are watching her. Even after she agrees to spy on Sebastian and goes so far as to marry him in support of her masquerade, the film shows little interest in her gaze, amatory or professional, and none at all in the ways she looks at the two men who are watching her. Practically the only time when Alicia, who has been recruited to spy on Sebastian, actually watches him as closely as both the men in the film constantly watch her is the moment just before they meet at the riding club.

Even in the very next scene, when they meet for cocktails, she is less visually attentive to Sebastian, from whom she repeatedly looks away, than she is hyper-aware of his scrutiny of her. And why not? Since she already knows most of what she needs to know about him, her paramount concern is to insinuate herself into his confidence by reassuring him that she can be trusted. Alicia neither needs nor wants to look at Sebastian. Instead, her comportment echoes that of countless painted nudes summarized by John Berger's dictum: "Men look at women. Women watch themselves being looked at."[23] Even more to the point, nothing Alicia sees in this scene or at any time thereafter until the very last sequence of the film gives her pleasure. She cannot possibly be happy to hear Sebastian describe his "hunger" to see her again to or to catch a glimpse of the government agent Prescott, whose sudden appearance with his wife at a nearby table reminds her both of what her business is with Sebastian and how far beneath Mrs. Prescott she must seem.

When Sebastian's colleagues kiss Alicia's hand on her first visit to his house, she is allegedly paying close attention to who they are and how they look so that she can pass information about them on to Devlin and his colleagues—for example, a description of Dr. Anderson that allows them to identify him as "Professor Wilhelm Otto Renzler." But the oppressively tight close-ups of their heads as they bend over her hand shift the emphasis from her gaze to theirs, which seem to seize and pin her with a nightmarishly ritualistic fervor. When the film emphasizes Alicia's attentiveness, she is always attending to physical details—the locked closet, the telltale bottle of wine, the key to the wine cellar—that define her relationships with these men rather than watching the men themselves. Even, or especially, as a spy, Alicia remains an object of the gaze rather than a master of it. Her own point-of-view shots never express power or desire but only the insecurity, amounting in her case to an entirely justified general paranoia about the opposite sex, that she imputes to Devlin. Joe McElhaney acutely notes that by the time the Sebastians poison her, "Alicia's face has lost almost all its capacity to be a functioning Hitchcock face, which is to say that it has lost its ability not only to connote the act of looking but (always its corollary in Hitchcock) the act of thought and perception."[24]

Notorious is the first of Hitchcock's films to explore the connection between the professional insecurity of amateur spies and the sexual and emotional insecurity that characterizes virtually all of his leading men. This exploration replaces the ocularcentricity Martin Jay ascribes to post-Enlightenment French thought with an "ocular-*ec*centricity" that "is the antidote to privileging any one visual order or scopic regime."[25] The common element that links the insecurities of the characters in *Notorious* is the inability to accept oneself as other people see one. Alicia typically deals with this problem by casting her eyes downward, Devlin by shifting his eyes left and right or letting his eyelids droop, Sebastian by refusing to look at the people he is condemning to death. This inability to accept the identity other people's gazes confer on one, which will become the great subject of *Psycho,* expresses itself here as an occupational neurosis that amateur spies share with flirtatious lovers: the need for the power conferred by the gaze coupled with the inability to take responsibility for the act of gazing. The characters in *Notorious* repeatedly fail to look at each other because, much as they want to watch each other, they cannot bear the responsibility of watching.

5. Home-front spying. Before *Notorious,* Hitchcock's thrillers had alternated between domestic crime melodramas—typified by *The Lodger, Blackmail,* and *Murder!*—and the espionage tales that predominated in his Gaumont-British period—*The Man Who Knew Too Much, The 39 Steps, Secret Agent, Sabotage,* and *The Lady Vanishes. Notorious* fuses the two genres more tightly than any earlier Hitchcock film by its handling of the gaze.

Hitchcock from the very first had been fascinated by the specular gaze of voyeurs like the unnamed patron who watches the dancers at the Pleasure Garden through binoculars and a monocle, the male reporters who dog Larita Filton in *Easy Virtue,* the private detective (Theo von Alten) in *Champagne* (1928), and the uncredited cook in *Waltzes from Vienna. Shadow of a Doubt* is organized around symmetrical acts of spying in a domestic setting. In the first half of the movie, Charlie spies on her uncle with increasingly revealing results. In the second half, Uncle Charlie spies on Charlie with increasingly murderous intent. Both activities are tinged with a perversely sexual overtone. The quasi-romantic courtship of Uncle Charlie and his namesake is signaled most explicitly by Charlie's early ardent attestation, "We're twins. . . . I'm glad I'm named after you," establishing an identification her uncle uses to entrap her as she fights to deny it.

The link between spying and courtship that constitutes a perverse subtext of *Shadow of a Doubt* becomes explicit and inescapable in *Notorious.* It is the first Hitchcock film to make unmistakably clear the link between professional spying and voyeuristic spying that had been intimated as far back as *Champagne,* whose main action is framed by shots showing the point-of-view image of the mysterious private detective hired by the heroine's father through the bottom of the champagne glass from which he is drinking. In his Thirties films, the romantic foreplay of Hitchcock couples from Hannay and Pamela (Madeleine Carroll) to Iris and Gilbert had been defined more completely by squabbling than by either the predatory gaze of Jean Harrington (Barbara Stanwyck) in *The Lady Eve* (Preston Sturges, 1941) or the petty mutual surveillance of Jerry and Lucy Warriner (Cary Grant and Irene Dunne), the estranged couple in *The Awful Truth* (Leo McCarey, 1937). The next Hitchcock films to give any further intimation of the link between spying and sexual desire are *Suspicion,* in which Lina's gaze in the opening scene shifts from the impecunious stranger sharing her train compartment to the magazine that prominently displays a photograph of him, and *Mr. and Mrs. Smith,* in the sequences in which David Smith (Robert Montgomery) first stalks his estranged wife and then places himself in her path in order to win her back.

In *Notorious,* the anatomy of averted gazes, which systematically explores the links between espionage, seduction, flirtation, romance, and psychopathology, is complemented by its setting, which systematically links foreign to domestic intrigue. Even though it is a spy film set mostly in an exotic foreign land, *Notorious* is a stellar example of spying on the home front. The film never shows Devlin's home—in fact, it's hard to imagine Devlin having a home at all—and Alicia's house in Miami seems like temporary quarters. Alicia is no homebody, as her attempt to cook a chicken for Devlin reveals. Nonetheless, the film extends *Shadow of a Doubt*'s interrogation of domestic life onto the stage of international intrigue by focusing on the home life of spies. "It's odd," Alicia tells Sebastian over their first drink, "but I feel—at home with you." Her insinuating remark turns out to be even more ironic than she realizes, for once the locus of the film gravitates to the Sebastian home, it never truly leaves. As Alicia discovers when she returns from the honeymoon to find the house dark and the servants retired at Madame Sebastian's behest, his home has all the trappings of home except for hospitality, safety, and love. It might therefore seem, like the eponymous house in *Number Seventeen*, to be nothing more than a sham home, as Prescott's colleague Walter Beardsley suggests: "Sebastian's house is a cover-up for whatever this Farben group's up to here in Rio. We've got to get Miss Huberman inside that house and find out what's going on there." But the impatient Beardsley is on to a more profound truth than he realizes. The Sebastian home functions not only as a trap for the intruding bride it was initially intended to repel, but as a genuine expression of the relationships of its household members, who express their feelings by spying on each other. It is menacing not because it is fake but because it is real—as real as the Bates home in *Psycho*, which Norman Bates (Anthony Perkins) continues to maintain as a memorial to the domineering, much-loved mother he is convinced is a murderer.

As in *Shadow of a Doubt*, home is where the spying goes on. After experimenting in *Lifeboat* with an allegory that would represent a world war by a collection of excruciatingly representative types, Hitchcock tries something different in *Notorious*: narrowing the grand scale of *Foreign Correspondent* and *Saboteur* by focusing their conflict on the central insight of *Shadow of a Doubt*, that the most insidious spying is domestic spying. In both films, as in *Jamaica Inn, Rebecca,* and *Suspicion*, home, which ought to be a refuge from vicissitudes, becomes their heart and source instead. In all these films, home means someone else's home, even if it is where one lives. Charlie's alarm that her uncle has established himself in the Newton home and is in no hurry to leave is matched by the dawning realization of the second Mrs. de Winter and Lina Aysgarth that their husband's homes are not their own.

Secret Agent, the most thematically adventurous of Hitchcock's earlier spy films, had complicated what might have been a lightheartedly romantic look at spying by exploring the ways in which assuming the identity of a secret agent even in the name of the noblest cause could compromise not only the relationship between its hero and heroine, but their very humanity. *Notorious* sets the agenda for Hitchcock's later films by linking this exploration of what it feels like to be a spy to an exploration of what it feels like to be spied on. The corrosive power of the gaze on both its object and its subject becomes the great theme of Hitchcock's later films from *Under Capricorn* and *Stage Fright* to *Frenzy* and *Family Plot*. In lesser films like *I Confess, Torn Curtain,* and *Topaz,* the gaze remains institutional, with the notable exception of the puzzled but benevolent gaze of Sarah Sherman (Julie Andrews) in the first half of *Torn Curtain*; in the most characteristic of them—*Strangers on a Train, Rear Window, To Catch a Thief, The Wrong Man* (1957), *Vertigo, North by Northwest,* and *Psycho*—it is sexualized. Brandon and Philip's plan in *Rope* to torment David's family and friends by toying with their anxiety when he fails to show up at dinner is turned into an anatomy of their own behavior by Rupert Cadell. The pitiless gaze of the police investigators threatens to unman Manny Balestrero (Henry Fonda) in *The Wrong Man.* Spying games between potential romantic partners in *The Birds* yield to the global suspicion that the birds are watching from the jungle gym or the Brenner property as they prepare for their next attack. Out of all Hitchcock's later films, only *The Man Who Knew Too Much* and *The Trouble with Harry* are not subject to the empire of the gaze. *Esse est percipi*: To be, in Hitchcock's late films, is to be perceived by a watcher whose gaze, whether motivated by lust or fear, is inevitably malignant. It is a theme rooted in *Notorious,* from its very title to the Sebastian home.

6. Not fathers but mothers. The guiding spirit of the Sebastian home is Mrs. Sebastian—not Alex's wife, but his mother, who rules the roost, carries the keys, knows every one of her son's connections, and claims his ultimate allegiance. Although she is not the first of Hitchcock's maleficent mothers—she is preceded by Mrs. Whittaker (Violet Farebrother) in *Easy Virtue* and Mrs. Hillcrist (Helen Haye) in *The Skin Game* (1931)[26]—her appearance marks a turning point in Hitchcock's career. Families in Hitchcock's earlier films tend to be organized around fathers or father-figures and daughters. The obvious examples are the Father (Gordon Harker) and his daughter the Girl (Betty Balfour) in *Champagne,* Caesar Cregeen (Randall Ayrton) and his daughter Kate in *The Manxman,* Hornblower (Edmund Gwenn) and his daughter Chloe (Phyllis Konstam) in *The Skin Game,* Bob Lawrence and his daughter Betty (Nova Pilbeam) in *The Man Who Knew Too Much,* Colonel Burgoyne (Percy Marmont) and his daughter Erica in *Young and Innocent,* and General McLaidlaw (Cedric Hardwicke) and his daughter Lina in *Suspicion.*

Apart from the father-son relationship so central to *Waltzes from Vienna* and the more balanced families of *The Lodger, Blackmail, Rich and Strange,* and *Secret Agent,* Hitchcock's early films give special emphasis to such non-biological father-figures as the lecherous patrons of *The Pleasure Garden,* Fear o' God (Malcolm Keen) in *The Mountain Eagle* (1926), Mr. Verloc (Oscar Homolka) in *Sabotage,* Uncle Philip (Vaughan Glaser) in *Saboteur,* and Dr. Brulov (Michael Chekhov) in *Spellbound.* Even romantic leads like Farmer Sweetland, Frank Webber, Sir John Menier, Max de Winter (who admonishes his bride, "Can't be too careful with children"), and of course Uncle Charlie come across as father figures to the younger women who are paired with them in amatory patterns that induce more and more queasiness. Fathers in these films root their impressionable daughters or daughter-figures in institutional authority, often opposed, like Colonel Burgoyne, to forbidden fantasies of crime and romance. Father-figures who also happen to be lovers combine authority and romantic fantasy in more equivocal ways that these films explore ever more boldly.

Notorious begins as if it were going to be another such exploration, for the most important relationship its opening scenes establish is the one between Alicia Huberman and the

Figure 14

father whose conviction marks the climactic stroke in the tarnishing of her reputation. When Devlin arrives unannounced and uninvited at her party, he treats her like a child. The recording he plays of the scathing dialogue in which she chooses her adopted country over her father merely installs a new set of father-figures represented by Devlin and Prescott. The scene in which Devlin announces her father's suicide and she mourns the man he once was before "it all went to pot" makes it clear that he is taking her father's place as her handler, the man for whom this time she does agree to spy. Her relationship with the much older Sebastian smacks even more of fathers and daughters, especially since the romantic rivalry between the two men is charged by their status as representatives of rival regimes who use her as a pawn in their struggle for political control.

But if *Notorious* begins as another story of father and daughter, it ends as a story of mother and son. Alex may be the power behind Alicia's disappearance from her park bench, but the power behind Alex is his mother, who is more resourceful, more decisive, and more ruthless (fig. 14). Her unexpected prominence in the second half of the film makes

Sebastian more prominent as well, and more sympathetic, for he becomes the prize over which his wife and mother fight. His relationship with his mother makes his betrayal by Alicia and his revenge on her more personal than if he were merely acting on behalf of the Fatherland. His divided loyalties, dramatized so sharply in the film's final sequence, amount to a flaw that humanizes him more than Devlin. And putting him under the thumb of his mother emphasizes the genetic component to his nature—how did Alex come to be the way he is? just look at his mother for the answer—that never arises in the case of Devlin, who is given no family, no past, no reason for being the emotionally stunted lover he is.

The turn from fathers to mothers in Hitchcock is closely linked to the new importance of contested or fraught domestic spaces, for homes are the logical battleground for fighters who are defined by their relationships with their mothers. Ben Hecht, who along with Selznick had undergone psychoanalysis before starting work on *Spellbound,* was presumably attuned to the formative importance Freudian therapists assigned to relationships between mothers and sons. All the leading collaborators would have been aware of Philip Wylie's *Generation of Vipers* (1942), whose headline-grabbing accusation of "momism" as the root of myriad American social maladies made it a best-seller. It is hardly surprising, then, that Hitchcock, whose own mother had died in far-off England only three years before the production of *Notorious,* should have been more mindful than ever of mothers, and should have used them as both genetic explanations of his flawed heroes and pathologies of culture.

What is surprising is that once this pattern had taken root in Hitchcock, it persisted till the end of his career, beginning with a thoroughgoing critique of fathers and fatherhood. Although Manny Balestrero plays a more pivotal role as father than his wife Rose (Vera Miles) does as mother in *The Wrong Man,* his fatherhood is pivotal precisely because the suspicion under which he has fallen calls his authority within his family into question. In the 1956 remake of *The Man Who Knew Too Much,* the kidnapping of Hank McKenna (Christopher Olsen) forces his father Ben (James Stewart), who has been long accustomed to setting the rules for his family, to temper his authority by learning to cooperate with his wife Jo (Doris Day), whose feelings and ideas he suddenly realizes are as important as his own. Metaphorical fatherhood is similarly challenged in *I Confess,* which sets the institutional authority of the justice system personified by Inspector Larue (Karl Malden) against the personal authority of Father Michael Logan, whose questionable authority as "Father" is at the heart of the film. How authoritative can Father Logan be when he acts suspiciously, when he may be a murderer, and when he has certainly been romantically involved with Ruth Grandfort (Anne Baxter), whose husband Pierre (Roger Dann) represents an institutional authority of his own?

The fathers in *Stage Fright* and *Strangers on a Train* are utterly unable to rein in the dotty mothers with whom they are paired. Fathers are absent from *To Catch a Thief, The Trouble with Harry, North by Northwest, Psycho, Frenzy,* and *Family Plot,* whose mothers thereby assume new prominence in setting an agenda or assuming responsibility for their children. In *The Birds,* Lydia Brenner (Jessica Tandy) speaks wanly of her late husband, who could enter his children's world in a way that his widow knows she cannot. Madame Sebastian ushers in a host of variously threatening mothers whose sons are firmly under their mothers' thumbs. The most searching anatomy of this relationship is *Psycho,* whose murderer feels himself literally possessed by the dead mother who condemns his every attempt to declare his independence from her. But these "mama's boys," as Leonard Leff and Ina Rae Hark call them, also include Bruno Anthony (Robert Walker) in *Strangers on a Train,* Roger Thornhill in *North by Northwest,* and Mitch Brenner (Rod Taylor) in *The Birds.*[27] Even when mothers appear only for a moment, as in *Frenzy,* or are kept offscreen entirely, as in *Rope,* their mere mention invokes their power over their sons, a potentially menacing power that provides the comical ending in *To Catch a Thief* when Francie Stevens (Grace Kelly), having pursued John Robie (Cary Grant) to his bachelor home, tells him, "So this is where you live. Why,

Mother will love it here!" —provoking a wry look from him that ends the film.

More threatened still are families from which the father has disappeared, leaving an untrammeled mother in charge. The obvious example is *Psycho,* but even though no other mother in Hitchcock can match the malignity of Mrs. Bates, Lydia Brenner in *The Birds* and Bernice Edgar (Louise Latham) in *Marnie* both act to restrict their children's freedom and, at least in Mrs. Edgar's case, calamitously stunt their growth. Only the love of the aggressively paternalistic Mark Rutland (Sean Connery) rescues Marnie Edgar (Tippi Hedren) from repeating Norman Bates's fate of spending her entire life struggling in vain to win her mother's love, the lack of which Melanie Daniels (Hedren) bemoans in *The Birds.* Even *Family Plot* can be read as a fable about the calamities that follow when a family is headed by a matriarch like Julia Rainbird (Cathleen Nesbitt), whose desire for justice and peace is stronger than her judgment.[28]

The switch from fathers to mothers inaugurated by *Notorious* represents a switch from institutional to personal authority and from social to genetic theories of causality. More fundamentally, it signals Hitchcock's new interest in questioning authority through a series of psychological anatomies. The man-on-the-run genre poses an implicit challenge to the institutional authority of the justice system by proposing that not everyone the police deem guilty is really guilty. But this challenge is far more intensified in *Notorious,* where the authority in question is personal, psychological, and maternal; where it is rooted in the hero's or heroine's home; where it is felt as an oppressive regime of being watched; and where its violence does not erupt suddenly in a spectacular outburst but lingers as a pervasive, potentially lifelong force.

It offers, finally, more complex terms for negotiating questions of power. Hitchcock's later films are not only about the experience of being watched; they are about the crushing experience of being watched by Mother. Hitchcock's ongoing anatomy of patriarchy and its discontents has been amply documented. But this anatomy, searching as it is, is complemented by the films' sensitivity to the sovereign power of mothers and the cost of internalizing maternal norms. The Professor (Leo G. Carroll), the CIA, the patriarchal heads of Mount Rushmore that watch Roger Thornhill can give him awkward moments because they are so powerful, but only his mother (Jessie Royce Landis) can make him feel the comic agony of being ridiculed, just as only Norman Bates's eternally living image of his mother can make him feel psychotically consumed by guilt. When Richard Hannay wrestles with institutional power, the result is an exterior struggle that can be staged as an adventure. When Madeleine Elster wrestles with the ghost of her great-grandmother Carlotta Valdes or Norman Bates with the ghost of his mother, however, the interior can only be suggested by exteriorized images that leave it open whether Madeleine and Norman are actually possessed by their mother figures or if they are using madness to evade responsibility for their own crimes.

As *Vertigo* proceeds to its inexorable conclusion, Scottie realizes that Madeleine's apparently obsessive behavior was dictated not by her possession by the mysterious mother-figure Carlotta Valdes, to whom she was not actually related, but by the transformation of Judy Barton into Madeleine at the hands of her lover Elster, that pillar of patriarchy—a transformation Scottie has been only too eager to repeat. Hitchcock's deepening anatomy of patriarchal power in his later films is only the most celebrated example of his use of melodrama to illuminate social and emotional pathology. His later films consistently use physical violence to represent psychological trauma, prefer dramatic irony to mystery, cultivate a tone at once complex and unified, anatomize the expressive power of the averted gaze, scrutinize the relations between spying and domestic romance, and examine the consequences of internalizing maternal norms. *Notorious* marks the first time in Hitchcock's career when all these devices expressively converge. In setting the agenda for the masterpieces that would follow, it is truly Hitchcock's pivotal film.

Notes

I gratefully acknowledge the many editorial suggestions of Richard Allen and Sidney Gottlieb that I have incorporated into an earlier draft of this essay.

1. In "Alfred Hitchcock," Lindsay Anderson called *Notorious*, along with *The Paradine Case* and *Rope*, "the worst [film] of his career." See Anderson (1949), rpt. in *Focus on Hitchcock*, ed. Albert J. LaValley (Englewood Cliffs: Prentice-Hall, 1972), 48-59, at 57.

2. See Leonard J. Leff, *Hitchcock and Selznick: The Rich and Strange Collaboration of Alfred Hitchcock and David O. Selznick in Hollywood* (New York: Weidenfeld and Nicolson, 1987), 205-06.

3. Charles Barr, *English Hitchcock* (Moffat: Cameron and Hollis, 1999), 11.

4. Donald Spoto, *The Dark Side of Genius: The Life of Alfred Hitchcock* (Boston: Little, Brown, 1983), 289.

5. Keane's remarks about the film's fairy tale elements frame her audio commentary to the DVD of *Notorious* (Criterion Collection, 2001).

6. Robin Wood, *Hitchcock's Films Revisited* (New York: Columbia University Press, 1989), 153. Emphasis in original.

7. Excerpted in *Once Upon a Time . . . Notorious*, dir. David Thompson (Folamour/TCM, 2009).

8. Eric Rohmer and Claude Chabrol, *Hitchcock: The First Forty-Four Films*, trans. Stanley Hochman (New York: Ungar, 1978), 84.

9. Deborah Knight and George McKnight, "Suspense and Its Master," in *Alfred Hitchcock: Centenary Essays*, ed. Richard Allen and Sam Ishii-Gonzáles (London: BFI, 1999), 107-21, at 115.

10. Hitchcock's pleasure at making the audience long to intervene directly in the story is illustrated by his story of Joseph Cotten's wife (Patricia Medina) whispering to her husband as she watched Lars Thorwald (Raymond Burr) appear in the hall as Lisa Fremont (Grace Kelly) was going through his room in *Rear Window*, "Do something, do something!" See François Truffaut, with Helen G. Scott, *Hitchcock*, rev. ed. (New York: Simon and Schuster, 1984), 73.

11. Todd McGowan, "Hitchcock's Ethics of Suspense: Psychoanalysis and the Devaluation of the Object," in *A Companion to Alfred Hitchcock*, ed. Thomas Leitch and Leland Poague (Chichester: Wiley-Blackwell, 2011), 508-28, at 513.

12. Hitchcock, "'Stodgy' British Pictures" (1934), rpt. in *Hitchcock on Hitchcock*, ed. Sidney Gottlieb (Berkeley: University of California Press, 1995), 168-71, at 169.

13. Truffaut, *Hitchcock*, 69.

14. See *Memo from David O. Selznick*, ed. Rudy Behlmer (New York: Viking, 1972), 268-69, and Leff, *Hitchcock and Selznick*, 124.

15. Thomas De Quincey, "On the Knocking at the Gate in *Macbeth*," *Collected Writings*, new and enlarged edition, ed. David Massey (Edinburgh: Adam and Charles Black, 1890), 10: 389-94, at 389, 392, 393.

16. Susan White, "A Surface Collaboration: Hitchcock and Performance," in *A Companion to Alfred Hitchcock*, 181-97, at 186.

17. Interviewed in *Once Upon a Time . . . Notorious.*

18. Sidney Gottlieb, "Hitchcock's Silent Cinema," in *A Companion to Alfred Hitchcock*, 255-69, at 264.

19. The scientific and anthropological literature on looking and being looked at is vast. A good introduction that does not ascribe different patterns of behavior to men and women is D.R. Rutter, *Looking and Seeing: The Role of Visual Communication in Social Interaction* (Chichester: Wiley, 1984).

20. Richard Allen, *Hitchcock's Romantic Irony* (New York: Columbia University Press, 2007), 100.

21. Tania Modleski, *The Women Who Knew Too Much: Hitchcock and Feminist Theory* (New York: Methuen, 1988), 60.

22. John Orr, *Hitchcock and Twentieth-Century Cinema* (London: Wallflower, 2005), 110.

23. John Berger, *Ways of Seeing* (Harmondsworth: BBC/Penguin, 1972), 47.

24. Joe McElhaney, "The Object and the Face: *Notorious*, Bergman and the Close-up," in *Hitchcock Past and Future*, ed. Richard Allen and Sam Ishii-Gonzáles (New York: Routledge, 2004), 64-84, at 77.

25. Martin Jay, *Downcast Eyes: The Denigration of Vision in Twentieth-Century French Thought* (Berkeley: University of California Press, 1993), 591.

26. Michael Walker, *Hitchcock's Motifs* (Amsterdam: Amsterdam University Press, 2005), 307-08.

27. See Leff, *Hitchcock and Selznick*, 181, and Ina Rae Hark, "Hitchcock Discovers America: The Selznick-Era Films," in *A Companion to Alfred Hitchcock*, 289-308, at 303.

28. Interestingly, this motif is even stronger in Victor Canning's novel *The Rainbird Pattern* (New York: Morrow, 1973), which the film adapts.

Deborah Thomas

Family Dramas in *Hitchcock's* Stage Fright

Had Elizabeth's opinion been all drawn from her own family, she could not have formed a very pleasing picture of conjugal felicity or domestic comfort. Her father captivated by youth and beauty, and that appearance of good humour, which youth and beauty generally give, had married a woman whose weak understanding and illiberal mind, had very early in their marriage put an end to all real affection for her. Respect, esteem, and confidence, had vanished for ever; and all his views of domestic happiness were overthrown . . .

Elizabeth, however, had never been blind to the impropriety of her father's behaviour as a husband. She had always seen it with pain; but respecting his abilities, and grateful for his affectionate treatment of herself, she endeavoured to forget what she could not overlook, and to banish from her thoughts that continual breach of conjugal obligation and decorum which, in exposing his wife to the contempt of her own children, was so highly reprehensible.

Jane Austen, *Pride and Prejudice*[1]

If the title of Hitchcock's film *Stage Fright* announces at least one of its concerns—the fear of appearing in a role on stage and not getting it right—then the opening shot of the film, where a safety curtain goes up on London, makes clear that the stage in question is life itself. Indeed, a reluctance to play conventional everyday roles is the defining trait of Commodore Gill (Alistair Sim). He not only takes pride in being a small-time smuggler (and is thus the antithesis of "Ordinary" Smith [Michael Wilding], the film's representative of male conventionality, whose work involves bringing lawbreakers to justice), but has abandoned his wife and daughter to live on his own. If Smith is "ordinary" (a designation he admits to enjoying), then Gill is "Unique, quite unique," as he describes himself when asked what sort of a father he is. On the surface, at least, his idiosyncrasies appear positive and his humorously indulgent relationship with his daughter Eve (Jane Wyman) marks a significant change from the more usually oppressive parental and pseudo-parental paradigms in Hitchcock's films.

As the quotations from Jane Austen included above are meant to suggest, an illuminating prototype for the relationship between Eve and her father is that between Elizabeth Bennet and her father in *Pride and Prejudice*, where, similarly, the father has withdrawn (at least as far as his library) from a foolish wife and domestic irritation while maintaining a gently ironic appreciation of his daughter at the expense of his wife. However, despite the reader's complicit pleasures in the husband's critique of his wife and his appreciation of his daughter's good sense, we—with Lizzy Bennet—are made well aware of the cruelty implicit in such a position, as the second of the two quoted paragraphs above makes clear. The train of thought which leads from the first quoted paragraph to the second, which almost immediately follows on from it in Austen's novel, shifts blame for the Bennets' domestic disharmony from the mother's foolishness to the father's scorn, placing such shifts of thought well within the bounds of Elizabeth's awareness, despite the third-person prose.

Eve Gill is less astute and aware than her literary predecessor, and considerably more naïve, but the film itself is not. Consider the speech Eve is in the process of making when Jonathan (Richard Todd) intrudes upon her on the RADA rehearsal stage: "No, papa, you are cruel. If all parents were of your mind, marriage would be an impossibility, and then what would become of the human race?" Indeed, I shall argue that Eve's relationship with her father and its complex ramifications are central to the project of the film, which moves Eve not only from play-acting a life of danger and excitement to settling for one of safe domesticity, but also from identifying with her father to identifying with her mother (Sybil Thorndike). The shifting of guilt for the murder from Charlotte (Marlene Dietrich) to Jonathan plays a central part in the development of this dynamic, as does the shifting of Eve's emotional commitment from Jonathan to Smith.

It is extremely difficult to untangle the precise circumstances surrounding the murder of Charlotte's husband, which we learn of through an assortment of versions, including: (1) Jonathan's lying flashback, (2) Charlotte's elliptical conversation with Freddie, (3) her dressing-room conversation with Jonathan, (4) the set-up conversation when Eve pretends to blackmail Charlotte, and (5) Jonathan's confession to Eve in the stage-set coach, not to mention Commodore Gill's guesswork version. Once Jonathan's lies have been admitted and excised from his original account, a few things become unambiguously clear: Charlotte was present at the murder, though the actual killing was committed by Jonathan; her dress was splashed with a little blood, but a larger bloodstain was added by Jonathan some time later.

The events' uncertainties circle around the extent of Charlotte's moral involvement in the crime and Jonathan's motivation in enlarging the stain, the ostensible sign of Charlotte's guilt but, more importantly, the *actual* sign of Jonathan's betrayal of her to save his own skin (this attempt to pin the crime on her occurring well before he supposedly becomes aware, as he later tells Eve, of her alleged betrayal of him). Jonathan claims he did this to make Eve believe his story, but he clearly does so at Charlotte's expense. All versions of these events agree upon (or offer no alternative to) the fact that Jonathan brought Charlotte a clean dress from her house (where her husband lies dead) to Jonathan's flat, where she waits in the slightly bloodied dress. So Jonathan's only opportunity to bloody the dress further is after Charlotte leaves him with the dress in his own apartment well away from the murdered man. The question perhaps arises as to whose blood he uses to do this: presumably, his own, though this is never made explicit.

Such questions of plausibility are of little interest to Hitchcock, of course, and hardly occur to the viewer embroiled in the considerable intricacies of the plot. Nonetheless, in view of what I shall argue, there is a pleasing symbolic resonance in taking the spilt blood as belonging to no specific man, since Charlotte's "crime," in Jonathan's eyes (or so he says), is her betrayal of *him*, and Commodore Gill's reference to Jonathan as "Ruined, and by a woman!" could as well refer to his feelings of betrayal at his own wife's hands as to Charlotte's betrayal of either Jonathan or her husband. The husband supposedly murdered at Charlotte's hands becomes a stand-in for both Jonathan and Gill, a "blood-brother" to them both, from their shared perspectives as men who consider themselves to have been ill-used by women. That Gill later uses his own blood to stain the doll's dress, which he carries inside his jacket in a manner similar to Jonathan's hiding of the actual dress when he eluded the police in his flashback, is surely telling here. Charlotte's guilt is constructed first by Jonathan, whose lying version of events implicates her as her husband's murderer, and second by Gill, with whom the idea of her framing Jonathan as the killer originates.

The fact that Commodore Gill projects onto Jonathan aspects of his own history is suggested by his comment to Eve that "You've roped him but he's not yet broken to harness, is that it?" So it is not just Charlotte but his daughter Eve herself whom he places in opposition to Jonathan (and, symbolically, himself). In this context, it is worth noting that Eve's stage father at the RADA rehearsal exclaims, "Stab me if ever there was such an ungrateful child," shortly before Eve's speech about his cruelty to which I've already referred, thus placing

Eve in the role of ungrateful child, just as her actual father's "roping and harnessing" imagery places her in the role of potential wife/domesticator. In both cases, it is the father (whether on stage or off) who defines the child's ingratitude or the domesticating woman's oppressiveness and who construes himself as victim. It should be remembered that, when Gill smears his own blood on the doll to incriminate Charlotte (a wife), he does so on a doll which is a simulacrum of a child (a daughter), suggesting that, for Commodore Gill, no female—of whatever age—can be trusted. Assuming Gill had some say in choosing his daughter's name, its evocation of the biblical Eve and her legacy of universal female guilt makes his cynicism about women and girls alike even clearer.[2] Gill's relation to Eve is part of a complex network of mutually mirroring relationships, and his encouraging her to defeat Charlotte and exculpate Jonathan is ambiguous at best, symbolically serving needs of his own both to disparage his wife and to vindicate his own marital irresponsibility.

This may help to explain the consistency with which Gill concocts plans which are not merely extremely cruel to Charlotte (especially given that she turns out to be innocent of the murder, if not completely blameless in goading Jonathan to perform the actual killing, at least according to Jonathan himself, though we never know the extent of her complicity for sure). Such plans are also extremely dangerous to Eve. "She *might* murder *you*," he tells his daughter, shortly after he's admitted, "I'm beginning to enjoy this," and his concern over her involvement is nominal at best, and certainly short-lived. The plan to confront Charlotte with the bloody doll in order to plant the idea of Charlotte's guilt in Smith's mind does nothing of the kind, serving rather to expose Eve (in her guise as Charlotte's maid) to his watching eyes. The scene where Eve attempts to blackmail Charlotte is, once again, orchestrated by Gill, but it only elicits Charlotte's admission that she was present at the murder. It leads on, however, to Jonathan's arrest, Eve's attempt to help him hide, and her father's realization (via Smith) that Jonathan is the killer after all. Gill's calling out to Eve that Jonathan is the murderer, precisely when she is alone with Jonathan and he too can hear her father's words, puts her at far greater risk than she would otherwise have been.

Charlotte's real "crime" is in her lack of regret at her husband's death. "He was an abominable man. Why do women marry abominable men?" she says in Jonathan's flashback, its inclusion there indicating its significance to Jonathan, no doubt, although it is also consistent with Charlotte's attitudes elsewhere and can be taken, arguably, as accurate enough. More generally, Charlotte is a threat to the film's male protagonists (especially Jonathan and Commodore Gill) in her lack of emotional attachment to *all* men—her unruffled refusal to give them any importance—of which her composure at her husband's death is a specific instance, but only one of several. Her indifference to Jonathan is explicit and lies at the root of his sense of betrayal (though she wishes him well enough and, in Eve's words, "was glad he got away"). She is equally cool with Freddie (and he with her), belying Jonathan's claim that "I was to kill her husband and leave the coast clear for that Freddie Williams." Charlotte was casually involved with Jonathan while still a married woman; there is no reason to believe an involvement with Freddie would require her husband's death either. If she wishes her husband dead, one presumes it is to be rid of an excessively unpleasant man, and not to replace him as husband with anyone else, having learned her lesson the first time round. Her musical number at the theater ("The Laziest Girl in Town") is further commentary, perhaps, upon her boredom at the attentions of men. Thus,

> When I kiss they want some more,
> And one thing more becomes a bore,
> It isn't worth the fighting for . . .

and so on.

That men matter less to Charlotte than women do is further evidenced in the way in which she models all betrayals upon the hypothetical loss of her mother's love. As she tells Sergeant Mellish (Ballard Berkeley), who is keeping an eye on her after Eve's misguided attempt at blackmail: "When I give all my love and get back treachery and hatred, it's . . . it's as if my mother had struck me in the face." This, to her, would be the ultimate betrayal. This pivotal sequence presents itself as a moment of revelation, when we will learn the truth about Charlotte at last. Having just discovered that Mellish has overheard and taken down in shorthand everything she's said to Eve in the dressing room, Charlotte nonchalantly smokes and eyes his notebook: "It's not all in there."[3] However, although we are thus prepared to hear the truth, what follows, taken at face value, is scarcely coherent. Indeed, Charlotte's assumption, which leads into her account, that the overhearing of her conversation with Eve has exposed her as an accessory to murder, is itself unconvincing, since Charlotte was adamant in insisting to Eve throughout their overheard conversation that "I was there in the room when Jonathan killed my husband . . . but I had nothing to do with it. . . . It's the sacred truth. I swear to you it is." So why is she now so quick to describe herself as an accomplice to Mellish when nothing she's said to Eve is actually incriminating?

Further, it is not at all obvious what we are to make of her story about the dog she loved who hated her back: "At last he bit me, and I had him shot."[4] Are we to assume the dog is somehow analogous to her husband, and that he was the one to whom she gave all her love and got back "treachery and hatred . . . as if my mother had struck me in the face"? Nothing we observe of her suggests strong feelings of love for her husband; in any case, even if she loved him once, in the past, why wait until now to have him killed? Aren't her implied serial infidelities and indifference sufficient payback? What exactly is the true account she purports to give to Mellish?

The only way I can begin to make sense of this scene is to take note of the two instances in the film where Charlotte is most seriously rattled: when she's shown the bloodied doll at

Figure 1

the garden party (fig. 1) and when she discovers the police have listened in on her conversation with Eve (fig. 2). Both these moments confound her in the almost "magical" way they appear, from Charlotte's point of view, to be conjured up out of the blue: Who on earth has sent her the doll? Who on earth is Eve, if not who she's said she is, and why has she delivered Charlotte up to the police? Both events are sudden inexplicable threats that seem to materialize from nowhere. They act to reposition her for an instant as a wide-eyed and bewildered child whose world no longer makes sense, and they may suggest that the "as if" in her statement about her mother may be a decoy for a maternal betrayal or withdrawal of love that has actually occurred and is now being remembered and repudiated at the same time. Is this the truth that Mellish's notebook does not—cannot—contain? Are the stirrings of reawakened childish hatred in response to such maternal betrayal (akin to the response to a biting dog) the cause of her overly hasty acknowledgment of present guilt? The film is too reticent and evasive for us to be sure. However, it is certainly plausible that, just as Commodore Gill uses Eve to enact symbolic family dramas of his own, so too may

Figure 2

Charlotte be caught up in a situation which evokes and reworks a traumatic past. If Eve simultaneously plays wife and daughter in her father's schemes, so too may Charlotte-as-child continue to inhabit and co-exist with her adult self.[5]

A possible residue of early childhood—and certainly a striking aspect of Charlotte's character—is her lack of pretense. Even when Jonathan's good-will is essential to her safety, she is unambiguous in her refusal to make promises she has no intention of keeping ("Well, you don't want me to give up everything, do you?"), and we have only Jonathan's word on any contrary behavior towards him in the past. This honest contempt for men may be a bit too close to the bone for Commodore Gill, who, in the context of his own life, "never hoped to be appreciated," as he tells Eve. "Yes, your mother cured me of that. That's why I never could be bothered with your mother." At this stage, Eve's pat reply—"*I* appreciate you, father"—firmly allies her with him in his antagonism towards her mother and, thus, in his plan to help Eve vindicate Jonathan by shifting his guilt onto Charlotte, a displaced version of his insufficiently appreciative wife.

It is ironic that Eve, while allying herself with two men (Jonathan and her father) against two women (Charlotte and her mother), should use feminist rhetoric to further her plans. Thus, posing as a journalist, she tries to convince Charlotte's maid Nellie to let her take her place by arguing, "Well, we women reporters have a tough job competing with the men, especially on important stories like this." Nellie, however, is bitterly aware of the use Eve is making of her and the superficiality of her role-playing, telling Eve, "I see. All you got to do is to put on some of your old clothes and make yourself look common, like me." Eve's mother too, in a rare moment of clear-sightedness, sees through the disguise without even realizing there is one (the fact that Eve's mother's reading glasses form part of Eve's "costume" as Nellie is a further link between mother and maid; Eve herself, however, is virtually blind in the glasses, amply suggesting her lack of any critical perspective on her own behavior). More poignantly, when Detective Inspector Smith politely— and, one presumes, falsely—tells Mrs. Gill that he's heard a lot about her, the need for reassurance in her eager response ("Oh, have you? Is Eve very fond of me?") is indicative of the extent to which she feels unsure of her daughter's affection and left out of the alliance between Eve and her father.

However, Eve's worst transgression against her own sex is to be found in her deceiving Charlotte, at her father's suggestion, as we've noted, with Eve posing as a blackmailer in order to elicit a confession. The scene builds out of Charlotte's most sympathetic moments, and those where she seems, however fleetingly, most sincere in her concern for Eve. Charlotte commiserates, "You must be tired too. It can't be easy to be a dresser when you've had no experience. But you're quite good. Very good indeed." Following this praise, she tells her, "I like you. You're so very sweet and patient. I don't suppose I'm easy to get on with," and then gives her some extra money and offers her a lift. Her manner is genuine and motherly, in contrast to

Figure 3

her cool irony elsewhere. The fact that Eve reveals her double-dealing to Charlotte at precisely the point when the latter is presented as a caring maternal figure brings home the ways in which Charlotte functions as a displaced version of Eve's mother against whom her father seeks to recruit her on his side. Although much earlier she'd told her father, "But *you're* my audience. I wish you'd give me a little applause now and then," she only receives this recognition now, following her feigned attempt to blackmail Charlotte, as he claps silently (fig. 3).

The disturbed expression on Eve's face, however, is evidence of her growing uneasiness and barely conscious guilt at having played the role required for his approval. This moment—the bringing together of Eve's duplicity towards a sympathetically maternal Charlotte with her father's applause and her own half-puzzled distress—is a turning point in the film. It is soon to be followed by Commodore Gill's endangering of his daughter's life (by his revelation of Jonathan's guilt within the latter's hearing) and Eve's turning on Jonathan in order to save herself.

Before we look at the ending of the movie (Jonathan's death and Eve's departure with Smith), another crucial moment

Figure 4

needs examining. I have been arguing so far that the film follows a path whereby Eve and her father are complicit in a plan to discredit Charlotte which, in some sense, can be read as re-enacting, in displaced form, a family drama in which Eve is enlisted by her father to take symbolic revenge upon her mother, whose "victim" he perceives himself to be, Gill identifying with both Jonathan and Charlotte's husband in their implied ill-usage at Charlotte's hands. This is further complicated by Eve's supposed love for Jonathan, which her father sees in terms of imagery of entrapment ("roping and harnessing"), thus linking her in Gill's mind to his wife. So Eve is potentially an object of her father's hostility, as well as his ally, a supposition his endangering of her seems to confirm.

What I am maintaining, of course, is that the *film* makes such a reading plausible, and not that the characters themselves are presented as conscious of such psychodynamics. Eve's disturbed expression after her attempt to push Charlotte to an admission of guilt reveals at most some glimmerings of awareness of her impossible situation (fig. 4). If her father identifies with Charlotte's husband and with Jonathan, Eve can hardly identify with her mother and with Charlotte, against whom she has been positioned (both literally and

Figure 5

symbolically) by the alliance with Jonathan and her father. She is adrift with no anchor in the narrative world, acting out interests which are not her own. The eventual solution to her dilemma is "Ordinary" Smith, though this is far from clear-cut, as we shall see.

We have looked at the turning point in the movie where Eve shifts from deceiving Charlotte to falsely reassuring Jonathan before abruptly revealing his presence to the police in order to save herself. Now we must examine a second, earlier turning point that collaborates in this realignment of her loyalties: the moment when it becomes clear that Eve is not in love with Jonathan but with Smith. The scene in question is, ironically, the point at which Jonathan comes nearest to transferring his own affections from Charlotte to Eve, having arrived at Eve's house after his conversation with Charlotte in the dressing-room. As he embraces Eve, telling her, "Oh, darling, I know I should never have trusted her," Eve is unresponsive, looking over his shoulder at the piano which Smith had played earlier that day, the point made even clearer by the reprise of his music on the soundtrack.

The earlier scene when Smith first plays the piano for Eve and her parents (fig. 5) places Smith on the left, Mrs.

Gill (seated and looking off-screen) on the right, and the conspiratorial father and daughter in between them. The camera movement out from Eve and Mr. Gill to include them all emphasizes both Eve's position as her father's accomplice and also the way in which not only her mother but Smith as well is pushed to the periphery by this alliance. Having invited Smith to tea, however, Eve is dismayed when she notices her father's presence, a first sign of resistance, perhaps, to their alliance and her false position within it. An ominous close shot of the back of her head blocking her father from our view as she exclaims in consternation, "Father, what are you doing here?", suggests the shift away from her father which the developing relationship with Smith will require. As Smith plays the piano, Mrs. Gill remarks, more aptly than she knows, "Oh, it's just like Sherlock Holmes and his fiddle. A stream of beautiful sound and then, suddenly, up pops the solution." Later that day, caught in Jonathan's embrace, Eve remembers the "stream of beautiful sound," and the transference of her emotional attachment to Smith ("the solution") is assured. The scene immediately following, when Eve and Smith kiss in the taxi, merely provides an opportunity for Eve to enact what she has already imaginatively affirmed.

Jonathan's turning away from Charlotte has led to Eve's turning away from him. She now wishes to tell Smith everything. Her father, however, on learning that she has not yet got Smith to suspect Charlotte (precisely because she was too busy becoming romantically involved with him), prevails upon her not to confess until their plan to discredit Charlotte—which exposes Eve to Smith instead—has been put into play. As it dawns on Smith that Eve has been playing the part of Charlotte's maid, he stares at the bloodied doll, which underlines my earlier suggestion that it is Eve's guilt as much as Charlotte's that the doll represents. Eve's father has learned that she is "changing horses in midstream" (and thus moving away from himself as well as from Jonathan by her involvement with Smith), while Smith now knows that he has been duped. Eve's growing loyalty to Smith is in clear conflict with her loyalty to her father, though for the moment both men may well feel led astray. Smith becomes aware, during his subsequent visit to Eve's house, that Jonathan is hiding out there, and he arranges for his arrest. Although he allows Gill's plan for Eve to pretend to blackmail Charlotte to go into effect, he has no doubt of Jonathan's guilt. Following Eve's pretended blackmail of Charlotte, when she helps Jonathan to hide at the theater and Smith tells Gill of the danger his daughter is in, Gill at last relinquishes his belief in Charlotte's guilt, though further endangering Eve by calling out in Jonathan's hearing that his guilt is known. As a logical consequence of Smith's view finally prevailing, Eve turns on Jonathan and, apparently compassionate and willing to help him escape, she betrays him to a brutal death. So the move from Eve's belief in Charlotte's guilt to her belief in Jonathan's is linked to the transference of her emotional commitment from Jonathan (and her father) to Smith. As the movie ends, Smith—and not her father—leads her away from the scene.

This account may seem to imply that Smith is more positive than is actually the case. That Hitchcock movies generally take a cynical view of romance is evidenced by the sexual politics of the romantic relationships in many of his other films, but such a view is also specifically signalled here by the obvious illusoriness of the stage-set Cinderella coach in which Eve's final conversation with Jonathan—where she expresses compassion for him in order to save herself—takes place. More to the point, a negative image of Smith's future with Eve may be hinted at when she pretends to faint in order to help Jonathan escape after his dressing-room confrontation with Charlotte. As Smith's surrogate, a fellow policeman, goes to her aid with a look of some resignation, Eve grasps him tightly round the neck, her eyes shut, while he attempts to prise her fingers free, the scene ending with an emphatic fade

Figure 6

as he makes the attempt (fig. 6). But most particularly, Smith himself is a man who takes pride in being ordinary, and who says of his professional opinion that Jonathan is guilty, "We're inclined to accept the obvious as being obvious." His view of the world is, therefore, very much embedded in common sense and, as a result, is strongly conventional in its ideological assumptions. In contrast to Jonathan and Commodore Gill, whose hostility to women clearly demonstrates that all is not well between the sexes, Smith accepts the surface world of which Hitchcock's films are such a consistent critique.

Eve herself seems at odds with Smith in a number of her comments throughout the film. For example, she tells him in the pub, "I wonder what Charlotte Inwood is really like. *Really*, I mean," and then later, in the taxi, "After all there must be a lot that doesn't appear on the surface, I mean, like wheels within wheels. Who . . . who knows what goes on in a woman's mind. I don't know." In a sense, in investigating Charlotte, Eve is investigating herself and her own mixed motives (one may readily compare this with the female narrator's fascination with Rebecca as she tries to

Figure 7

find out more about her in Hitchcock's 1940 film of that name). Having identified at that point with her father's and Jonathan's view of Charlotte as a dangerous *femme fatale*, she has had to suppress her own experience and the capacity to identify with and understand Charlotte and, thus, aspects of herself. The two men see a darker side to Charlotte, but one which Eve, by her positioning, is unable to demystify and reinterpret (in, say, feminist terms). By the time Eve has switched her loyalties from Jonathan and Gill, however, Smith is waiting in the wings, ensuring she look no further than Charlotte's—and her own—surface innocence, rather than to resentments towards men and longings for maternal love which, though unenacted, may still persist below the surface or even break through. In Eve's final conversation with Jonathan, where he finally confesses his guilt, the lighting highlights their eyes (fig. 7), as Eve confronts the truth about Jonathan face to face (including the fact that his first victim was female, and that he now intends to kill Eve). In marked contrast to this, Smith, after Jonathan's death, turns Eve away from the scene, hiding her face and leading her away into the

Figure 8

shadows as the movie ends (fig. 8). We anticipate a future of conventional marriage where no significant questions will be asked. Given the marital breakdown of Eve's parents, however, Hitchcock's film is hardly optimistic about this prospect.[6]

It is tempting to generalize from the analysis of this movie to Hitchcock films as a whole. Is it the case that his male characters elsewhere are also split into two camps? On the one hand, we may find men who are unconventional and dangerous and see women as the enemy, and, on the other hand, those who are conventional and safe and are predominantly in conflict with other men (pursuing them as fugitives from the law, for example). This would seem to presuppose a "normal" world of male rivalry and antagonism, where conflicts between the sexes are suppressed by an ideology of romantic love and marriage, and a dangerous and unconventional counter-world which calls such assumptions into question, uncovering hostilities between the sexes which may take shape as shared male misogyny (like the "blood-brotherhood" of Commodore Gill, Jonathan, and Charlotte's husband). Where an unconventional hero himself betrays such resentments towards women (as in *Notorious*, for example), his transforming them into conflicts with other men (especially with the villains) may be a process closely linked to that whereby he is himself conventionalized. These possible readings of the Hitchcock *oeuvre* as a whole must remain speculative in the present context but are worth further thought.

I began this account by offering up the possibility that the film's title betrays an anxiety about the playing of conventional roles (particularly in the context of the family, but, as we have just seen, within romantic relationships as well), and not just a fear of participating in the literally theatrical. We have seen how the ostensible romantic hero and the ostensible good father are rendered dubious in contrasting ways that circle around Eve and her uncertain position between them. Hitchcock, further, seems to implicate himself as well, first by slyly casting his own daughter Patricia (then a RADA student like Eve and, also like her, the Americanized daughter of a mischievous and ironic Englishman) in the minor role of "Chubby" Bannister, the character's name seeming to exhibit his capacity to joke at his daughter's expense. Further, however, Hitchcock implicates himself in his treatment of *us*, betraying our trust with the famous lying flashback with which the film more or less begins. If we can't trust our parents—if we can't trust the director as parental surrogate—then whom can we trust? Where one has a right to expect to be safe, one finds betrayal and lies (thus, the irony of Jonathan's being killed by a *safety* curtain, just after Eve has lulled him into a false sense of security; thus, Charlotte's experiencing all betrayals as akin to a mother's slap; thus, more elliptically, the fact that Jonathan's uncontrollable rages go back to childhood). In view of all this, the patter of the duck-shoot concessionaire (Joyce Grenfell) at the charity garden party as she tries to drum up business—"You *are* sorry for the orphans, aren't you?"—is pointed indeed. In Hitchcock movies, those *with* parents are most to be pitied. This moment provides the most delicious irony of the film.

Notes

1. Jane Austen, *Pride and Prejudice* (London: Penguin, 2003), 228.

2. Indeed, we are alerted to Gill's facility in coming up with suitable names for people when he comments on Nellie Goode's surname at the charity garden party: "I could think of lots and lots of much more appropriate names for you."

3. Charlotte's comment has its equivalent in *Marnie* when Mark (Sean Connery) informs Mrs. Edgar (Louise Latham) that he's going to tell her daughter Marnie (Tippi Hedren) what really happened to her when she was a child, and Mrs. Edgar replies: "Oh, no you won't, mister, because you don't know the whole story. And nobody does but me."

4. *Marnie*'s counterpart to the biting dog is Forio: Mr. Garrett, with whom Marnie boards her beloved horse, tells her that "He tried to bite me twice already this morning," and Marnie ends up shooting Forio. However, there is never any indication of hostility between Marnie and her horse, and she shoots him out of compassion when he's been injured. Nevertheless, both Forio and the biting dog may be seen to function as objects of displaced emotions from elsewhere.

5. This is yet another link with *Marnie*, though Marnie's recovered childhood memory is much more explicit than Charlotte's wide-eyed reactions and vague explanation to Sergeant Mellish, where the full story never quite surfaces. Unlike Charlotte, Marnie discovers that her mother did love her after all.

6. As Michael Walker points out in his account of the film, "There are quite a few Hitchcock films which end with the heroine "going off with" a policeman . . . and in almost every case the ending seems in important respects unresolved or uneasy." See "The Stolen Raincoat and the Bloodstained Dress: *Young and Innocent* and *Stage Fright*," in Richard Allen and Sam Ishii-Gonzalès, eds., *Alfred Hitchcock: Centenary Essays* (London: BFI, 1999), 196.

CHARLES BARR

"The Knock of Disapproval":
Juno and the Paycock *and its Irish Reception*

Although it was well received in some quarters at the time of its release in 1930, Hitchcock's film of the play by Sean O'Casey, *Juno and the Paycock*, has attracted little interest or enthusiasm since then. Two recent works by Irish scholars that one might have expected to give it some attention brush it aside contemptuously. For Christopher Murray, in his definitive biography *Sean O'Casey*, it is "quite atrocious," while for Adrian Frazier in *Hollywood Irish* it is "inept" — not a word that has often been applied to Hitchcock.[1] This dismissal is in spite of the fact that the film brings us so much closer than any other surviving records could do to O'Casey's play as performed by the actors of the time, including Sara Allgood, who had created the part of Juno at the Abbey Theatre in Dublin, and whose career both before and after her move to Hollywood is one of the main topics in *Hollywood Irish*. Other Abbey figures in the cast include Maire O'Neill (Allgood's sister), Sydney Morgan, and — albeit in a small part — another of Frazier's subjects, Barry Fitzgerald. Revulsion must indeed be intense if it leads both these authors to pass over such an apparently significant resource. Neither author is a film specialist — they are Professors of Drama and Literature respectively — but film scholars, including Hitchcock scholars, have been scarcely more positive. Michael Walker, in his comprehensive analysis of *Hitchcock's Motifs*, dutifully cites instances from this film in appropriate places — the index has twelve entries for it, under eight different headings—but has described it to me as "the only Hitchcock I actively dislike and find hard to watch."[2]

Little of substance has been written on it.[3] Consistent with this, my own treatment of it in *English Hitchcock* was fairly brief, ending with a summarizing reference to "the disjointed hit-or-miss quality of a film that seems likely, even allowing for the very different expectations of that period, to have worked better as a learning experience for Hitchcock and his technicians than as an experience for cinema audiences."[4] Since then, however, a period of living and working in Dublin has increased my interest in the whole question of Hitchcock's Irish connections, and has given scope for research in some excellent Irish archives. This case study of *Juno and the Paycock* draws upon those resources, and is intended as a step towards a fuller study not exactly of "Irish Hitchcock"—though he was indubitably at least quarter-Irish, via his maternal grandfather—but of "Hitchcock and Ireland."

The aim here, then, is not to rehabilitate the film as a neglected masterpiece, which would be difficult, or even to offer a fresh textual analysis, but to place it in a fuller context: what has been underestimated is not so much the film itself as the influence that the experience of its making and reception can be seen to have had upon Hitchcock, at a transitional stage of his career.

The play's setting is Dublin 1922, during the same Civil War period that is dramatized, from very different perspectives, in the later stages of both Neil Jordan's film *Michael Collins* (1996) and Ken Loach's *The Wind that Shakes the Barley* (2007); the conflict is between "Treatyites" who are ready, with Collins, to accept the terms negotiated in London for limited independence, and "hard-liners" opposed to this. Johnny Boyle was active in the earlier fight against British rule, losing an arm, but has broken with his hard-line former comrades, and taken refuge in the family home in Dublin, living with mother Juno, work-shy father Jack ("Captain"

Boyle, the Paycock of the title), and sister Mary. In the course of the play, the family spends money in expectation of a legacy, which falls through; Mary is deserted by her English lover, Bentham, and left pregnant; and Johnny is hauled away to be executed. Juno is left to mourn and, it is implied, to leave with Mary.

Hitchcock told Truffaut and others that he had not found an effective way to take the play over and turn it into good cinema: the contemporary praise for it embarrassed him.[5] Two factors clearly had an inhibiting effect: his intense admiration for the play itself and the technological context in which the film of it was made. Taking the latter first, the film undeniably has a cumbersome and "stagy" feel to it, as a result, primarily, of the extreme newness and rawness of the apparatus for recording synchronized dialogue, which imposed severe restraints on cinematic style. Although the film is always dated 1930, it was shot in 1929 and had its first showing at the end of that year, so it is a very early sound film, and moreover one made in England, which was still struggling to catch up technically with developments in Hollywood.[6] Compare that other film of the same moment based on a respected text, the war play *Journey's End* by R.C. Sherriff: the three main figures behind the filming were all British—Michael Balcon, George Pearson, and the play's West End stage director James Whale (here making his film debut)—but it was shot in Hollywood, taking advantage of sound-film resources that were superior to anything Balcon could yet offer at Gainsborough.[7]

Hitchcock had worked closely with Balcon, and would do so again, but he was now at British International Pictures (BIP) with John Maxwell, who had been quicker to install and exploit sound technology.[8] The most spectacular result of this was, of course, *Blackmail*, made immediately before *Juno* but much less stagebound, and incomparably, and for good reason, more celebrated and written about both at the time and since. The circumstances of its production are too well known to need relating here; the two major differences from its successor are that it was conceived and begun as a silent film, with extensive and mobile non-dialogue passages retained in the sound version, and that the original play by Charles Bennett did not have anything like the success or prestige of O'Casey's. Hitchcock and his collaborators were able to adapt it freely, drawing out the strong cinematic potential already built in to it, and including moments of bold experimentation with sound. While it does have some long and painfully slow dialogue scenes, these don't dominate the film or compromise its impact.[9]

In contrast, Hitchcock was committed from the start to respecting, as far as possible, the integrity of O'Casey's text and of its theatrical structure and setting, just as Whale and his collaborators were in the case of *Journey's End*. The play had been a major success first at Dublin's Abbey Theatre in 1924 and then in London in 1925, where it ran for a long time and had, as in Dublin, several early revivals.[10] It became the first instance of the strategy for play adaptation that Hitchcock would come to articulate, and now and then to practice, notably—and inevitably, by then, with greater finesse—in *Rope* and *Dial M for Murder*: if you buy the rights to a strong piece of theatre, respect its theatrical confinement rather than "opening it up."[11] The play itself was the selling point, all the more so at this early stage in dialogue cinema when the literate spoken word was such a strong attraction in its own right. I perhaps underestimated this factor in discussing the film in *English Hitchcock*.

Hitchcock had got to know O'Casey, who was by now based in London; he consulted him in the preparation of the film, and had plans for future collaboration. When the project was announced, it was naturally big news in Ireland, a country which had little history of indigenous film production. Dublin especially, with its high rate of cinema attendance, would offer a significant market for the film, and anyone associated with the theater would watch carefully to judge how it had been done. Lady Gregory, charismatic co-founder of the Abbey Theatre, herself a playwright and a devoted patron of O'Casey, saw the choice of the play for one of the first British talkies as a cause for all-round congratulations, as she wrote in a letter to O'Casey in April 1929, after the contract had been signed. He at once reported to another correspondent that

> I got a letter from Lady G this morning saying how glad she was that Juno was to be filmed, & that I—and Ireland—and the Abbey are to be congratulated that it is the first—or one of the first filmed for the talkies. Which shows that she & Ireland—and the Abbey are far more interested in it than I am.[12]

It does not seem that she, or indeed her co-founder W.B. Yeats, poet and playwright, and still a board member, ever actually saw the film when it emerged. She died in May 1932 at the age of 80, but until near the end was still traveling regularly to Dublin and elsewhere from her home in the West, Coole Park, and could have seen it had she chosen to. However, she wrote to Sara Allgood early in 1930 that "I don't think I will go to hear you on the talkies—I would rather keep these lovely intonations in memory, unspoiled by any medium."[13]

Lady Gregory's statement captures the attitude of Dublin theater people, unimpressed by the new talkie medium, but very aware of it. Initially, Hitchcock had made all the right moves. Having got O'Casey on his side, at least temporarily, and convinced him of his respect for the text, he focused on the settings. The publicity booklet for the film's London premiere reported that

> Mr. Hitchcock went over to Dublin in order to search for "local colour" and to arrange details of setting. Accompanied by Mr. F.J. McCormick, the versatile Abbey Theatre actor, who scored a great hit in the Abbey presentation, Mr. Hitchcock visited various areas in the city and collected material and scenes, and photographs were also taken of the "interiors" of several houses.[14]

Figures 1 and 2. Dublin tenements reproduced at Elstree: Juno and her daughter Mary, outside and inside.

This is one of only two visits by Hitchcock to Ireland for which I have so far found firm evidence.[15] The Dublin visit in September 1929 is reported in the local newspapers, but sadly without any photographs or any interview, nor do we know how the visit was fixed up: perhaps through O'Casey, or by having Hitchcock or the studio contact the Abbey and asking them to supply an escort. McCormick was an interesting choice, a man widely regarded already as the finest Irish actor of his generation, one who mainly held aloof from cinema until his much-praised role in Carol Reed's Belfast-set *Odd Man Out* in 1947; he died soon after it. In *Juno*, he had created the role of "Joxer" Daly, Captain Boyle's garrulous sidekick, but was evidently not considered for the film, which drew only on actors who were by now based in London, nor probably would he have wished to be, since he was so busy at the Abbey.

But other elements of casting were more contentious: this became just one of the controversies that came to surround the film. I will deal with these under four main headings: O'Casey's Involvement, Casting, Censorship, and Reception.

O'Casey's Involvement

The biopic based loosely on O'Casey's early life, *Young Cassidy* (1965, begun by John Ford and finished by Jack Cardiff, from a script by John Whiting), dramatizes his relationship with, among others, Yeats and Lady Gregory; it ends with his departure to England, so there was no scope for including his subsequent encounters with Hitchcock, which could have been interesting. O'Casey and Hitchcock were certainly an odd couple, the former open and impulsive (and turning out, from 1939 onwards, a succession of vivid autobiographical volumes), the latter much more guarded in every way. Retrospective testimonies never come with a guarantee of full accuracy, and these two men were, in their different styles, notably prone to self-serving, or simply absent-minded, distortions. It is no surprise that there are inconsistencies in the accounts given by them, or on behalf of them.

On 13 August 1930 the Dubliner Joseph Holloway (discussed below) referred in his diary to a social evening at a friend's house:

> Mr. Hughes told us of the introduction of O'Casey to Hitchcock after the "Juno and the Paycock" film was completed, and all O'Casey said was "Are you the bloody fool who turned down the world's finest comedian?"[16]

This hearsay account, referring to Barry Fitzgerald, may—possibly—give an authentic sense of the hostility by then felt by O'Casey, but it is quite wrong in implying that this would have been a first meeting. According to John Russell Taylor, in the authorized biography *Hitch*, their mutual friend Ivor Montagu

> engineered a meeting between Hitch and the playwright on the set of *Blackmail* . . . they immediately hit it off, and the deal to bring *Juno and the Paycock* to the screen, with some of the original Abbey cast, notably Sara Allgood as Juno, was soon finalized.[17]

Patrick McGilligan queries this, since O'Casey recalled watching a scene with Betty Balfour, which suggests that the film Hitchcock was shooting at the time was *Champagne*; this dating is supported by correspondence between O'Casey and

Montagu which did not find its way into the multi-volume *Collected Letters*.[18] O'Casey writes to him from his home in St. John's Wood early in 1928; the letter is undated, but Montagu sends a reply on 7 February of that year. O'Casey asks:

> a. Who are the best film producers in England? Hitchcock?
> b. If one gave a work to a film co would it entail a lot of work watching scenario and production?
> c. what companies here do the best work?

Montagu replies:

> a. I certainly think Hitchcock the most interesting.
> b. Depends. If you found a scenarist and director with congenial mind probably a few talks would get your point of view clear enough over to them, for them to get your meaning and go ahead. If they're not congenial you have to watch them every minute and then you'd break your heart.
> c. British International is good. Gainsborough is very good technically but too venal . . .

He then invites O'Casey to come with him to the BIP studios at Elstree: "six companies are working there, one of them Hitchcock's." At the time O'Casey is too busy to accept, but he writes again to Montagu on 6 May 1928; it seems that there have by now been some negotiations over filming *Juno*, and he wants advice. On 10 June, Montagu replies, explaining that he has "since been finding out the position. It is not, at the moment, a promising one":

> The point is that the director who wanted to make it is now employed by another company, and they have their fixed programme for him for at least a year ahead and do not want him to interrupt it. Nor, as a matter of fact, is his present company as ready to indulge him in *Juno* as the other might have been.

This seems to fit Hitchcock perfectly; he had seen and been impressed by *Juno* in 1925, he had moved from Gainsborough to BIP in 1927, and Gainsborough, having taken on the unlikely project of a silent adaptation of Noël Coward (*Easy Virtue*, his last film for them), might well have been more ready than BIP to consider a silent adaptation of O'Casey. Although Hitchcock has been named in the earlier letters, Montagu is no doubt being suitably cautious in not naming him now, but he invites O'Casey again to Elstree, where he knows Hitchcock to be working: "You mentioned in an earlier letter you'd like to see a film studio in full blast, would you still care to?" O'Casey replies, in terms that nicely express his ironic detachment from the medium, that next week is fine: "I could go with you to see how they gather together the things that astonish the people."

It is clear, then, that O'Casey met Hitchcock well in advance of *Blackmail*, that he was already aware of his standing in the industry, and that they had both been considering the idea of *Juno* as a silent film. But by the time the contract with BIP was signed in April 1929, with Hitchcock named as director, the studio's conversion to sound was well under way. It seems quite possible that O'Casey would have visited Elstree again while Hitchcock was engaged on *Blackmail*, as per Taylor's account, in which case he might have seen Betty Balfour again, shooting *The Vagabond Queen* on another set. More importantly, he would have had a chance to see the elaborate Dublin sets built for a film whose shooting overlapped with that of *Blackmail*: *The Informer*, directed by Arthur Robison, from Liam O'Flaherty's novel. That film's production history is very close to *Blackmail*'s, in that it was initiated as a silent film, but BIP made the decision, midway through shooting, to rework it for synchronized sound.[19] Who better to write the dialogue for it than O'Casey, who had just signed the contract for *Juno*, and who was so familiar with the city and its recent violent history? He was invited to do so, but declined, and the job was done instead by another playwright, Benn Levy, who did the same for the sound version of *Blackmail*.[20]

As for the *Juno* film itself, O'Casey later in life came to profess a blanket hostility to it (a travesty, nothing to do with me, never saw it), and his widow Eileen is used by Christopher Murray as an additional witness against Hitchcock: in her 1972 memoir *Sean* she called the failure to cast Barry Fitzgerald in the lead "an unpardonable artistic blunder."[21] Yet in a later conversation with Charlotte Chandler she did not mention this, insisting instead that he had been happy to write new lines for Fitzgerald to speak in his brief appearance in an initial scene as the Orator:

> Sean was pleased about Hitchcock's making the film, and he told Hitchcock to feel free . . . Sean was very cooperative and even wrote some new material for the opening scene. It was important that Hitchcock was the kind of director he was because there were some who wouldn't have gone back to Sean to make certain every word was his and to have him approve it.[22]

Taylor supports this, and even suggests that O'Casey wrote material for the scene that follows, set in the local bar, preceding the move into the single location of the stage play, the Boyles' apartment.[23] All of this is hard to reconcile with the animus that he later expressed.

It was perhaps their personal estrangement, soon after the filming of *Juno*, that led him to become so unhappy in retrospect, combined with the very mixed reception that, as we will see, the film had in Ireland. It is not in dispute that both men had been keen to go on working together. As Eileen recalled it, "My Sean was so overjoyed, he set about writing a new play that would be right for a Hitchcock film." Again, Taylor supports this: it seems to have been conceived as a screenplay, set in Hyde Park in the course of a single day, and only to have been turned into a play (*Within the Gates*) when the collaboration lapsed. According to Taylor, "some minor failure of communication—as simple as a misunderstanding about who should call whom—caused the project to fall by the wayside." O'Casey's version in *Rose and Crown* (1952) is less anodyne: he gives a disparaging account of the Hitchcocks' behavior as dinner party guests at the O'Casey home in London, at which Alma conveyed fastidious disapproval—the failure to follow up is blamed very much on her, and is resented.[24]

Casting

There was evidently never any question of doing any of the filming in Ireland, even for establishing shots of locations; obviously no sound facilities would have been available. Likewise, there was no plan to bring in actors from Ireland. Hitchcock was accurate in referring to his use of the "Irish Players," a kind of spin-off company now based in London, rather than the Abbey Theatre company itself.

As noted above, a main pretext for O'Casey's later hostility to the film was its failure to cast Barry Fitzgerald in the title role of Captain Boyle. This objection at first seems hard to argue with, in view of that actor's long and successful film career, and the fact that he had not only created the part at the Abbey in 1924, opposite Allgood, but had gone on playing it in every revival there. At the time, the case for using him was not so obvious. His film career did not start properly until 1936, when he went to Hollywood, along with other Abbey actors, to work on the John Ford film of *The Plough and the Stars*, and stayed on. Up to then, he had remained an Abbey regular, going to London only very occasionally: his first appearance there was a main role, on O'Casey's recommendation, in his new play *The Silver Tassie*, which had an eight-week run between 11 October and 7 December 1929, thus almost exactly coinciding with the production of the film of *Juno*. It was this that made him available to play the small role of The Orator at the start. He then returned to the Abbey, and was back in his accustomed part in the next revival of *Juno*, later in December.

Role	Abbey (1924)	London (1925)	Film (1929)
Juno Boyle	Sara Allgood	Sara Allgood	Sara Allgood
Capt Boyle ("The Paycock")	*Barry Fitzgerald	Arthur Sinclair	Edward Chapman
Joxer Daly	*F.J. McCormick	Sydney Morgan	Sydney Morgan
Mary Boyle	*Eileen Crowe	Kathleen O'Regan	Kathleen O'Regan
Johnny Boyle	*Arthur Shields	Harry Hutchinson	John Laurie
Mrs. Madigan	Maureen Delaney	Maire O'Neill	Maire O'Neill
Charles Bentham	Gabriel Fallon	Eric Page	John Longden
Jerry Devine	P.J. Carolan	David Morris	David Morris
Needle Nugent	Michael Dolan	J.A. O'Rourke	------------
(Mr. Kelly)	------------	------------	Fred Schwartz
The Orator	------------	------------	Barry Fitzgerald

Figure 3

Figure 3 shows the casting of the play respectively for the Abbey premiere, for the London premiere, and for the film. A few notes on the chart:

1. As Joseph Holloway noticed immediately, "Mr. Nugent (called Kelly in film) is made to be a Jew-tailor" — an undeniably distasteful caricature. This may have been a late decision, since Donald Calthrop (the blackmailer Tracy in *Blackmail*) was originally cast as "Needle Nugent," and some sources erroneously list him in that role. When O'Casey was challenged about this alteration much later by students writing from America, he angrily denied all knowledge of it.[25]

2. The onscreen titles misspell "O'Neill" as "O'Neil," and "Sydney Morgan" as "Sidney." (I failed to correct this in the Filmography of *English Hitchcock*.) The titles also list David Morris as Dave. The imdb.com website confuses both him and Morgan with others of the same name, suggesting that the film career of each was much more varied than in fact it was.

3. The four asterisks in the second column indicate Abbey actors who were brought to Hollywood by John Ford in 1936 for *The Plough and the Stars*, an equally contentious O'Casey

adaptation. Three of those four reappear in *The Quiet Man* (1952), filmed in Ireland and Hollywood. McCormick, married to Eileen Crowe, had died in 1948.

4. Of the total complement of actors, five worked with Hitchcock on other films. Sara Allgood had been in *Blackmail*, but is not, as Adrian Frazier and some others claim, in *Sabotage* as well. Of the Abbey cast, Maureen Delaney plays one of the kitchen staff in *Under Capricorn*. Of the non-Irish actors from the film, Chapman reappears in *Murder!* and *The Skin Game*, Laurie in *The 39 Steps*; Longden, like Allgood, had been in *Blackmail*, and reappears in *The Skin Game* and—by now in smaller parts—*Young and Innocent* and *Jamaica Inn*.

It is evident that, for the film of *Juno,* Hitchcock basically used the London cast which had impressed him so strongly in the theater, five of whom repeat their roles. Only Allgood is common to all three casts; this is because she had moved to London much more recently than the others, after *Juno*'s initial runs at the Abbey. Sinclair, Morgan and O'Neill had themselves worked at the Abbey for many years, but none of them since 1918. However, they remained recognizably Irish actors, as familiar with their roles as Fitzgerald was with his; indeed, Sinclair must have played the Paycock more times than he had. Hitchcock would undoubtedly have cast Sinclair for the film, alongside all the others from the London company, had he not committed himself to a provincial tour of the play.

So how about Fitzgerald? Holloway wrote this in his diary on 3 October 1929:

> Barry Fitzgerald tells in a letter to a friend that he is rehearsing night and day for O'Casey's play [*The Silver Tassie*]. Large sums have already been offered for seats on the first night . . . Fitzgerald is likely to appear as Capt. Jacky Boyle (his original part) and Sara Allgood (her original part) on the screen. Alfred Hitchcock wants them for the British talkie film of this play.[26]

A pasted-in newspaper cutting states that "Production on this is held up till Mr. Fitzgerald is available, and this is not possible until after 'The Silver Tassie' opens."

In the event, these practical difficulties were not overcome. The program for the film premiere noted that Hitchcock "had great difficulty . . . in casting the important role of Captain Boyle, Juno's good-for-nothing husband. Arthur Sinclair was committed to the Juno tour, while Barry Fitzgerald was among those rehearsing for 'The Silver Tassie.'" It went on to describe the dramatic last-minute discovery of Edward Chapman, acting at the time in a West End show with Gracie Fields. Hitchcock saw the show, tested him the next day, and signed him.

Was Fitzgerald tested as well, and rejected, as one source suggests?[27] Hitchcock's contrary explanation that Fitzgerald was tied up with rehearsing the play is plausible; but so was Sydney Morgan, and he did make it into the film. Morgan, unlike Fitzgerald, had long experience on the London stage, and of working with this company of players; but it was surely a greater challenge for Edward Chapman to fit himself in, since he hadn't even, as Fitzgerald had, worked with Allgood. Chapman was an English actor, with no Irish links and no film experience. His casting and his performance were not well received by Dublin critics, which is understandable since it is a labored one and the accent fluctuates uncertainly. But maybe Fitzgerald actually preferred to focus on making the most of his big first break in the London theatre, with its demanding "night and day" rehearsal schedule, and to take a small role in the concurrent film production rather than the taxing lead one. The first night of the play (11 October) came in the very same week in which *Juno* began shooting.[28]

Whatever the precise reasons for the casting, the debates about it are important in helping to explain the mixed reception of the film in Ireland, where critics and theatre people were fiercely loyal to Dublin actors—and why not, in the context of this very Dublin play? Vivid testimony here is provided by the diarist Joseph Holloway, a key figure in the

Figures 4 and 5. Barry Fitzgerald in the opening scene as the Orator; Sydney Morgan as Joxer Daly, Edward Chapman as Captain Boyle

city's film and theater culture of the time, architect of the Abbey Theatre building, and an obsessive chronicler of Dublin life and culture over many decades up to his death in 1944; he left an extraordinary legacy of over 200 volumes combining diary with scrapbook, held in the National Library of Ireland. A small percentage of the content has been published, but predictably with a focus on theater. Holloway has a lot to say about films as well.

When *Juno* opened in Dublin, he was provoked by a local newspaper's reference to the casting:

> I dropped a post card to M.A.T. (*Sunday Independent*) saying that "The statement in the 'puff' on 'Juno and the Paycock' that Kathleen O'Regan plays her original stage part of Mary Boyle amused me, seeing that that actress never has appeared at the Abbey Theatre where 'Juno and the Paycock' first saw the light of the stage. 'Puff' as much as you like my dear M.A.T. but please state facts correctly. Yours sincerely, Joseph Holloway." (18 July 1930)[29]

Holloway was right, but the Dublin-born O'Regan had been part of the original London cast, so M.A.T. was right as well. In a subsequent diary entry, Holloway could not bring himself to express any greater approval of other members of that

Figures 6 and 7. Maire O'Neill as Mrs. Madigan; Kathleen O'Regan as Mary Boyle.

London cast, praising only one of them, her identity predictable:

> I saw "Juno and the Paycock" at the Grafton. . . . Were it not for the final ten minutes of Sara Allgood's tragic acting as Juno I should have viewed the picture as a grotesque version of O'Casey's play. Maire O'Neill made Mrs. Madigan an excessively vulgar woman with a loud irritating laugh oft repeated, and a love for drink over-accentuated—so much so that she staggers about in a muddled condition at the impromptu party at Boyles. Morgan over-acts Joxer into a grotesque almost, and the English actor cast for Captain Boyle never convinces, and is never anything save a painfully exaggerated imitation of Arthur Sinclair's usual mannerisms . . . Sara Allgood looked very big in pictures—her voice recorded splendidly. Kathleen O'Regan's Mary didn't ring true, nor did the young actor's voice as Johnny Boyle, though he looked and acted the role of the haunted boy well. (25 July 1930)[30]

The diary reports many others as feeling the same, especially about Chapman, and Holloway was so much of an insider that I think we can see these comments on casting and performance as broadly representative of the Dublin intelligentsia's response to the film—and

Figures 8 and 9. John Laurie as Johnny Boyle; Sara Allgood as Juno Boyle, in the final scene.

trace a continuity between that and the dismissal of it by the two present-day academics cited at the start of this essay.

Censorship

Such was Joseph Holloway's insider status that he also held down the post of Deputy Film Censor for many years, on either side of the industry's conversion to sound. The published selections from the diaries, again, pay no attention to this strand in his life, but the unpublished material is full of detail. From these diaries, combined with the official censorship records available now in Dublin, we get a strong sense of the repressive forces to which Hitchcock's early films were subjected. While the film of *Juno and the Paycock* was itself untouched, partly in deference to the status of the widely-seen original—"I passed it without a cut. It seemed, as far as I could judge, to keep near to O'Casey's play, after some opening incidents" (Holloway, 7 February 1930)—there was, as we will see, a strong backlash, which a look back over what happened to its predecessors, *Blackmail* in particular, helps to explain.

Censorship in the still-young Irish Free State was exceptionally severe, and would remain so for decades.[31] The country was virtually a theocracy, in thrall to the Roman Catholic church, and there were no Adults-Only certificates: every film had to be innocent enough to be put before a mixed-age audience.

Hitchcock's silent films had a difficult time, which might be seen as ironic in view of his own Catholic background. Surviving censorship records do not go back as far as *The Lodger*, but its successor, *Downhill*, at once ran into trouble. Rejecting it, the censor recorded his reasons:

> Would this very unpleasant picture contribute anything to morality, art, or entertainment? I think not. It follows the downhill path of a boy, touching on seduction and adultery and other scenes from the cinema.[32]

"Scenes from the cinema," indeed! The medium is here simply equated with sexual license and depravity, and must be vigilantly controlled. Although the ban was lifted on appeal, subject to cuts, the appeal against the ban on *Easy Virtue* was rejected, and the ban on *The Manxman* was not even felt to be worth contesting; both films, after all, have "immoral" women at their center. In his diary, Holloway scornfully rejects the liberal arguments for passing *The Manxman*, arguments that had invoked the wide and uncontested circulation of the novel on which it was based, and he shows himself to be obsessed—not too strong a word—with the immorality of *Blackmail*.

Interspersed with the diary entries, he frequently pasted in or transcribed press cuttings, and picked up early reports on *Blackmail* from London, including a positive one in the *Irish Times* (3 July 1929): "It is hoped that Dubliners will not have to wait very long before having an opportunity of seeing the first British talkie and their own particular actress, Sara Allgood, in her first talkie role." The *Irish Independent* (24 June) had similar praise for the film and for Allgood, but also a reservation: "Mr. Alfred Hitchcock, who produced it at Elstree, has in the main a right to be satisfied. One scene is open to serious criticism as being unwholesome."

The scene is, of course, the long one in the artist's studio that leads up to the attempted rape of Alice, and her killing of the man in self-defense. Because of it, the Chief Censor,

James Montgomery, at first rejected the film outright in September, recording these comments on 2 December when asked to reconsider:

> As this was England's first big "Talkie" I thought I would bring it within the limits of a general certificate by cutting reels 4 and 5 in a very drastic manner. I pointed out to the Renter in my "Reserve Form 642" "Remember that this film is restricted to adult audiences in Great Britain and that such restriction is not enforced in Saorstat Eireann [the Irish Free State]." I re-viewed the film on December 2 and feel that this film even as cut is indecent and immoral. The attempted rape which is shown in a realistic manner is obviously the pivot of the play.[33]

Holloway agreed:

> At Eileen's, Miss Conroy said she saw a great film in London, "Blackmail." I said, Did you not object to young lady in artist's studio and her undressing? "Oh no—she didn't take off everything," was her reply. Aren't women the devils! (12 September 1929)

> I had a chat with Annie Allgood [Sarah's mother]. She asked me why "Blackmail" was turned down by the censor? And I told on her account of a very ugly "rape" scene in the artist's studio leading to murder of the artist & as the episode was vital to story the Censor had no option but turn it down. (4 December 1929)

But a few days after that conversation, to the displeasure of both Censors, the Appeal Board approved the cut version of the film. Soon after that, two members of the Board told Holloway they regretted the decision. The film by now was being "assailed on all sides. . . . in Australia the whole scene in the studio has been cut out—you only see the girl enter and leave the building" (3 January 1930). And he continued to assemble a range of reported reactions, for and against, including this nice piece of clerical prurience:

> Father Hooke saw "Blackmail" in London, and went into the Grafton while it was on at the critical moment when the lady was removing her garments. Two priests behind where he sat were amused at the way he timed the delicate situation. (26 January 1930)

A more ominous church viewpoint comes in an undated report pasted in later that year from the weekly Catholic journal *The Standard*, expressing indignation at attempts to weaken the rigor of film censorship:

> When we observe that the worst of all films exhibited in this country, "Blackmail," was passed by the appeal board against the censor's decision, we are driven to wonder whether there is a will, even when there is a way to protect the nation.

These controversies over *Blackmail* are echoed, even intensified, when the film of *Juno* is screened in Ireland.

Reception

Alert readers may have noticed that although Holloway as Deputy Censor passed *Juno and the Paycock* for exhibition on 6 February 1930, soon after its London opening, it was not publicly shown in Dublin until July, and moreover that he himself waited until then before recording his opinion of the acting. This double anomaly can be explained:

1. The censors' office still had only silent film projectors; they were waiting impatiently for Parliament (the Dail) to pass new legislation for the censorship of sound as well as visuals, and to supply the necessary equipment. This was not done until June 1930. Meanwhile, talkies like *Blackmail* and *Juno* were judged on visuals only, a ludicrous situation, as Holloway stressed

in a letter to an American friend which he transcribed, as usual, into his diary:

> We see talkies "silently" at Censor's office, and the effect is uncanny at times. The people "shadowed" on screen may be saying anything, but no sound reaches us, and their mouths opening and shutting look for all the world like fish out of water, gasping for breath. (7 March 1930)

Anything deemed offensive in *Blackmail* would have been picked up from the visuals, in contrast to *Juno*, in which Holloway understandably could see nothing provocative; nor could he yet judge the actors.

2. The day after *Juno* was passed, clearing it for its anticipated opening later that month at Dublin's largest cinema, the Savoy, the same cinema had a press show of the Hollywood film *Smiling Irish Eyes*. It was received with scorn as, in a representative review, "a wholly erroneous and unfavorable impression of Irish life and characters," based on demeaning stereotypes.[34] When the film opened, the screening was spectacularly disrupted by protests in which

> blows were exchanged. . . . A chorus of boohs and catcalls resounded through the house, completely drowning the voices from the film. There were cries of "Take it off" and "It's an insult," and the film was taken off and the lights turned on.[35]

The manager, Mr. Knott, an Englishman who had only recently taken over the job, agreed without much argument to withdraw *Smiling Irish Eyes*, but did not replace it with *Juno and the Paycock*. Instead, he set up at short notice a remarkable test screening:

> There were about 60 or 70 people present, including clergymen. . . . "I want your honest views about the film," he said, "I want to know if it is suitable for

showing here. . . ." He certainly did not want to present films that would be objectionable.[36]

Cards were handed out, asking the audience to judge the acceptability of *Juno* by voting Yes or No. Although the critics of Dublin's two leading papers, the *Irish Independent* and the *Irish Times*, were optimistic and gave reviews that were broadly positive, the manager did not go ahead with the film; either the voting figures were unpersuasive, or he was too nervous after the recent debacle. The ever-industrious Holloway records a vivid contemporary witness who evidently voted No:

> I was speaking to Mr. Martin who heard and saw "Juno and the Paycock" at the Savoy the other morning and doesn't think the Dublin public will stand for it. There is too much swearing and taking the name of the Lord in vain for Dubliners generally. He thought the singing of Sacred Heart of Jesus outside at funeral while others were swearing was most irreverent. Another came in and said "It was great," and then Martin and he had a sharp encounter. To have such films received with acclaim in the Free State is to give picturegoers all the world over the wrong picture of the Irish people. Martin was glad "Smiling Irish Eyes" got the knock of disapproval in Dublin, and he thinks that "Juno" will get the same. (February 1930, precise date not specified)[37]

On 3 March, Holloway reports the same Mr. Martin as saying that "no exhibitor has as yet taken the 'Juno and the Paycock' film—they all fight shy of it after the fate of 'Smiling Irish Eyes.' " In July, however, another central Dublin cinema, the Grafton, takes the plunge, puts it on, and is rewarded with good reviews and good houses: long queues are reported, and the booking is extended.

In October, the film plays in the Republic's second city, Cork, and an *Irish Times* columnist is struck by the different

Figure 10. Abbey Theatre actors waiting to see the film in Dublin, July 1930. At the center of the group are F.J. McCormick and Arthur Shields. Photo from the Arthur Shields Collection, courtesy of the Library of the National University of Ireland, Galway.

atmosphere there: "I had already seen the film in Dublin, and was struck by the quiet manner in which the Cork people received it."[38] There was perhaps something ominous here: when the Abbey production of the play visited Cork in 1925 they had been forced to make hasty changes to the text by theater representatives who "had taken grave moral exception to it."[39] In November, the Atheneum cinema in another major city, Limerick, in the West, announces its reopening, after converting to sound, in these terms:

The most up-to-date
Western Electric Company's Sound Apparatus
SPECIAL ATTRACTION Sean O'Casey's Classic
"Juno and the Paycock"[40]

They should have been more cautious, as Holloway could have advised them. His conversation with Annie Allgood about *Blackmail* has already been quoted; she went on to refer to her other daughter Molly (stage name Maire O'Neill) and her colleague, by now her husband, Arthur Sinclair:[41]

> She told me of the awful time Sinclair and Molly had in Limerick with O'Casey's plays. . . . [In *Juno*] Bentham had to be married to Mary Boyle, and "going to have a baby" had to be changed to "going to be a mother." . . . Many of the references to God and the Virgin in all three plays had to be eliminated. In fact they had an awful time of it altogether. (diary, 4 December 1929)[42]

Holloway mentions this exchange to a friend, who tells him "it was so dominated by religion down there that they would allow little to pass that took God's name in vain or had any tendency to cross the borderline of state morality."

It was this city of Limerick, even more sensitive than Cork, that was now giving a high-profile launch to a film version of the play which had *not* been thus bowdlerized, in which Mary was made pregnant outside marriage and her mother and the film made a point of not condemning her—and which was not free of verbal profanities, as Martin had so forcefully complained.

In hindsight, the outcome looks predictable. On 10 November, reels from the film were seized from the projection box and burned in the street. Ken Mogg has attributed this action to "Irish nationalists. . . . O'Casey's anti-extremist barbs had struck home."[43] This is not quite the right emphasis. The film had been provocatively denounced from the pulpit on moral grounds in advance of the screening, and another priest stood up in court for the main perpetrator (Stephen Kennedy, a local shopkeeper), testifying to his good character.[44] The *Juno* film was unacceptable in Limerick for reasons of sexual morality more than politics. It was replaced immediately by *The Virginian*, starring Gary Cooper.

What is more, the press reports of the burning led to copycat acts of violence. In Dublin, the protests feared early in the year by the Savoy manager now erupted:

> Wild scenes were witnessed at the production [*sic*] of the film "Juno and the Paycock" at the Sackville Cinema in Dublin on Sunday night.
> The moment the picture was put on an uproar began in the front of the building and there was boohing and cat-calls.[45]

That seems, understandably, to have more or less ended the dissemination of the film in the Republic; and it was too firmly anchored in that transitional moment of film technology, too close to a straight recording of the stage play, to last for long anywhere else, even though writers as diverse as James Agate and Lionel Collier had praised it extravagantly on its first showing.[46]

I would argue, finally, that the whole experience of the film of *Juno and the Paycock*—the struggle to turn it into proper "cinema," the tensions of the relationship with O'Casey, the troubled Irish reception—influenced Hitchcock in significant ways. He remained more respectful to O'Casey as a playwright than O'Casey was to him as a film-maker;[47] in structure, *Juno* is a fine example of the "well-made play" that became such an important model for him.[48] Critical reaction to *The Silver Tassie*, the play whose first run overlapped with the shooting of *Juno*, made much—whether in approval or otherwise—of the scenes in which actors chant lines in unison: this seems like a direct influence on the scene of jury discussion in Hitchcock's next feature, *Murder!* The basic concept of the scenario that the two were planning to develop together, the dawn-to-dusk story of Hyde Park, which later became the play *Within the Gates*, was one that Hitchcock later tried to revive with other writers, though he could never get far with it.[49] More positively, *Juno* also marked his first sustained engagement with political themes and politically motivated violence, and their effect on individuals and families, a structure with which he was to become so identified, starting with his "breakthrough" into the political thriller genre in 1934, *The Man who Knew Too Much.*

As his first 100% talkie, made at a time when dialogue was still hard to combine with freedom of camera style or of cutting, *Juno* had constrained Hitchcock to, as it were, make a virtue of necessity by devising a variety of strategies for long actor-centered takes, mostly with an element of camera movement; I describe some of these in *English Hitchcock*. Even then, it was possible to break long dialogue takes into separate shots by shooting with two or more cameras, and editing the results together; Victor Saville claimed to have used up to six cameras simultaneously for this purpose for scenes in *Woman to Woman*, another early-sound production which, like *Journey's End*, Balcon had dispatched to Hollywood.[50] But in *Juno*, Hitchcock preferred for most of the time to let dialogue shots run on: he would do the same in his next version of a high-prestige play, *The Skin Game*, and would famously, voluntarily, revert to precisely this minimal-cutting style years later—by then in a more nuanced way—for *Rope* and *Under Capricorn*. The *Juno* experience here was seminal.

At another level, *Juno* can be argued to have had a distinctly negative effect, in turning him decisively against Ireland, the country of his maternal grandfather's birth; by the time of his collaboration with John Russell Taylor on the biography, he was concealing any such connection altogether. Already, in advance of filming *Juno*, he must have been uneasily aware of the banning or heavy censoring in Ireland of several of his earlier films, *Blackmail* included, by a dominant culture whose Catholicism was much narrower than his own, and which was deeply suspicious of the very medium of cinema. But he then threw himself into filming O'Casey's play, touring Dublin with one great Irish actor, McCormick, and working closely on the film with others; he even devised his own cameo as a Dublin barman, later cut out as being potentially a distraction.[51] Then it all went sour: several months of nervous delay before showing the film, a condescending response from the Dublin intelligentsia, and finally the film burned in the streets in Limerick and booed off the screen in Dublin. And before or after that came the bitter break with O'Casey himself.

The one author to have touched seriously on Hitchcock's relation to Ireland is Patrick McGilligan. He speculates that the assassination in London in 1922 of an English military hero by Irish republicans, one of whom, Patrick Dunne, went to the same school as Hitchcock, made a profound impact on him and helped, along with the Johnny Boyle plot in *Juno*, to inspire and shape his vivid depiction of the "chaos world" of violence in later films.[52] This idea can perhaps be extended. Ireland stood in family terms for a past of poverty and hunger, in political terms for irruptions of violence, and in professional terms, after *Juno*, for rejection, even humiliation. We can both understand Hitchcock's disavowal of Ireland, and speculate on the effects of this disavowal on him and his subsequent work. These are themes that I hope to explore in a sequel to this essay.

Notes

1. Christopher Murray, *Sean O'Casey* (Dublin: Gill & Macmillan, 2004), 214; Adrian Frazier, *Hollywood Irish* (Dublin: Lilliput Press, 2011), 252.

2. Michael Walker, *Hitchcock's Motifs* (Amsterdam: Amsterdam University Press, 2005), 469. The quotation is from an email message, 25 October 2009.

3. Apart from brief accounts in the standard biographical and critical works, one can point to four more focused ones. Maurice Yacowar's chapter in *Hitchcock's British Films* (Connecticut: Archon Books, 1977) concentrates on the changes the script makes to the play text; Barry Monahan, in *Ireland's Theatre on Film* (Dublin: Irish Academic Press, 2009), concentrates on the handling of cinematic space. More widely circulated than either of these is James Morrison's essay, "Hitchcock's Ireland: The Performance of Irish Identity in *Juno and the Paycock* and *Under Capricorn*," in *Hitchcock: Past and Future*, Richard Allen and Sam Ishii-González, eds. (London: Routledge, 1999). Though theoretically ambitious, this essay is hard to take seriously because of its inexplicable insistence that the action takes place during the War of Independence rather than the Civil War that followed the Treaty, and that Johnny Boyle becomes a casualty in a struggle between Republicans and "Unionists"; nor, in discussing performance, is it any more sensitive to the technological context of early sound cinema than it is to the political context. A judicious wider view of the film, in relation to the play and to its author, is given in Jack Morgan's shorter essay "Alfred Hitchcock's *Juno and the Paycock*" in *Irish University Review* 24, no. 2 (1994): 212-16.

4. Charles Barr, *English Hitchcock* (Moffat, Scotland: Cameron and Hollis, 1999), 104.

5. François Truffaut, *Hitchcock*, revised edition (New York: Simon and Schuster, 1985), 69.

6. Jane Sloan mistakenly dates its release as June 1929, the month in which the sound version of *Blackmail* was first shown. *Alfred Hitchcock: A Filmography and Bibliography* (Berkeley and Los Angeles: University of California Press, 1993), 88. Shooting took place in October and November 1929.

7. The filming of *Journey's End* began in Hollywood in November 1929, while *Juno* was in progress at Elstree. The two films in fact offer many parallels. Both used one indispensable star from the first production (Colin Clive, Sara Allgood) along with a number of expatriate actors. Hitchcock, as we will see, drew on the London-based Irish Players, while publicity for *Journey's End* stated proudly that "the players . . . are all of Empire origin" (*Kinematograph Weekly*, 7 November 1929). Both films now feel dated and creaky, based mainly on faithful recording of dialogue and performance in long takes, with minimal "opening up," but this gives them all the more value as theatrical and filmic "time capsules," and as rites of passage in two distinguished directorial careers: James Whale in transition from stage to film, Hitchcock from silent to talkie cinema.

8. "The new 'sound' studios, which are rapidly nearing completion, will be fully equipped as sound-proof stages for the making of 'talking pictures'" (report in *Kinematograph Weekly*, 3 January 1929). As early as the 28 March issue, the paper's British studio correspondent, P.L. Mannock, is "interested to observe that sound accompaniments to 'Blackmail' are being experimentally made"; this is while the silent production is still in progress.

9. I argue the point about the play's built-in cinematic potential in "*Blackmail*: Charles Bennett and the Decisive Turn," in *Hitchcock at the Source*, R. Barton Palmer and David Boyd, eds. (New York: SUNY Press, 2011), 67-76. For a more detailed account of the formal parameters of *Blackmail*, see Barr, *English Hitchcock*, 78-97.

10. See Barr, *English Hitchcock*, 227, for a summary of this early stage history.

11. See, for instance, the discussion of *Dial M for Murder* in Truffaut, *Hitchcock*, 210.

12. David Krause, ed., *Sean O'Casey Letters, Volume 1, 1910-41* (London: Cassell, 1975), 344. Letter from O'Casey in London to Gabriel Fallon, 15 April 1929.

13. Lady Gregory, letter to Sara Allgood, 5 January 1930. Quoted with the permission of the Board of The National Library of Ireland, MS collections, file 15395 (3).

14. Program booklet accompanying the first run of the film at the Alhambra Cinema in London, January 1930, in the collection of the British Film Institute library.

15. The second visit was a brief touchdown in the West of Ireland en route from America to England. On 30 May 1946 the *Irish Times* carried a short item headed "Hitchcock to Make Film in Ireland," noting that "Mr. Hitchcock told our Shannon Airport correspondent that the film will be 'Under Capricorn,' from a novel by Helen Simpson. The opening scene is in Ireland in 1831, with Ingrid Bergman as the daughter of a British landlord." In the event, shooting was postponed until 1948, and no scene was set or shot in Ireland.

16. Joseph Holloway Diaries, National Library of Ireland, MS Collections. All passages from these diaries are quoted with the permission of the Board of the Library.

17. John Russell Taylor, *Hitch* (London: Faber, 1978), 104.

18. Patrick McGilligan, *Alfred Hitchcock: A Life in Darkness and Light* (Chichester: Wiley, 2003), 129. The O'Casey-Montagu letters come from papers donated by Montagu to the Museum of Labour

History in Manchester. They are quoted here courtesy of the Museum, and of Shivaun O'Casey, her father's literary executor.

19. Robison was unlucky, or simply not sufficiently prescient, in that the sound version of *The Informer* became a more awkward hybrid than *Blackmail*: dialogue comes in only towards the end, very abruptly, and is poorly voiced and dubbed. Yet up to then, and perhaps all through in the silent original, it is a powerful melodrama, in many ways superior to the Ford version of 1935, as Patrick Sheeran persuasively argues in *The Informer*, in the "Ireland into Film" series (Cork: Cork University Press, 2002). The Irish censor rejected it outright as an "impudent and mischievous distortion" of Dublin life in this same Civil War period; Ford's film, which transfers the action back into the War of Independence, would be rejected just as vehemently. See Kevin Rockett, *Irish Film Censorship* (Dublin: Four Courts Press, 2004), 92-93. All of this helps to bring out just how skillful Hitchcock was, first in his *Blackmail* strategy, and then in making his subsequent Dublin film acceptable there (at least in the short term).

20. "By the way, International Pictures wrote asking me to do the dialogue that is to go with 'The Informer,' but I turned the offer down." O'Casey to Fallon, in the letter quoted above (note 12). Krause's footnote identifies the film as John Ford's 1935 production. This obvious misinformation, a rare slip in a work of high-level scholarship, has since been widely disseminated.

21. Murray, *Sean O'Casey*, 489, quoting Eileen O'Casey, *Sean* (London: Macmillan, 1971), 105.

22. Charlotte Chandler, *It's Only a Movie: Alfred Hitchcock, a Personal Biography* (New York: Simon and Schuster, 2005), 74-76.

23. Taylor, *Hitch*, 105.

24. Eileen O'Casey, quoted in Chandler, *It's Only a Movie*, 76; Taylor, *Hitch*, 106; Sean O'Casey, *Autobiographies, Volume 2* (London: Macmillan, 1963), 353, quoted by both Murray and McGilligan.

25. David Krause, ed., *Sean O'Casey Letters, Volume 3, 1955-58* (Washington: Catholic University Press, 1989), 91-92. O'Casey's letter is dated 23 March 1955.

26. Holloway Diaries, NLI MS vol. 1929.

27. Gabriel Fallon, *Sean O'Casey, The Man I Knew* (London: Routledge and Kegan Paul, 1965), 134.

28. "Sean O'Casey's vivid Dublin comedy-drama begins this week," it was noted in *Kinematograph Weekly*, 10 October 1929.

29. Holloway Diaries, NLI MS vol. 1935.

30. Holloway Diaries, NLI MS vol. 1935.

31. Kevin Rockett's book *Irish Film Censorship* gives an admirably comprehensive historical analysis, based on access to primary documents.

32. Department of Justice files, 98/29/2. Reject book p. 92, judgment entered 31 May 1927.

33. Reject book p. 265. Rockett has more details of this case (*Irish Film Censorship*, 85).

34. *Irish Independent*, 8 February 1930.

35. *Irish Independent*, 12 February 1930. Kevin Rockett notes that those protesting included actor Cyril Cusack, then a student, and the subsequent distinguished historian and archivist of Irish film, Liam O'Leary; see Kevin Rockett, Luke Gibbons, and John Hill, *Cinema and Ireland* (London: Croom Helm, 1987), 53-55.

36. *Irish Independent*, 15 February 1930.

37. Holloway Diaries, NLI MS, vol. 1931.

38. *Irish Times*, 27 October 1930.

39. A vivid account of the confusion this caused to Sara Allgood and the company is given by Fallon, *Sean O'Casey, The Man I Knew*, 28-29.

40. *Limerick Echo*, 4 November 1930.

41. Their marriage in 1926 was Molly's second, her first husband, the journalist and diplomat G.H. Mair, having died at the start of that year. Earlier, she had been engaged to marry the Abbey playwright J.M. Synge before his premature death in 1909. Her life inspired the novel *Ghost Light* by Joseph O'Connor (London: Harvill Secker, 2010).

42. Holloway Diaries, NLI MS, vol. 1930.

43. Ken Mogg, *The Alfred Hitchcock Story* (London: Titan Books, 1999), entry on *Juno and the Paycock*, no pagination.

44. *Irish Times*, 25 November 1930. More details of the clerical opposition to the film in Limerick are given by Rockett, *Irish Film Censorship*, 396.

45. *Derry People*, 29 November 1930.

46. Collier, Review Editor of *Kinematograph Weekly*, called it "the best British picture we have yet seen," one that "ranks among the screen masterpieces of the world" (*Kinematograph Weekly*, 2 January 1930), and he was not a critic easy to please. Agate's review in *The Tatler* is quoted by Taylor: "*Juno and the Paycock* appears to me to be very nearly a masterpiece. Bravo Mr. Hitchcock! Bravo the Irish Players and bravo Edward Chapman. This is a magnificent British picture" (*Hitch*, 105-06).

47. The very last article O'Casey wrote, in 1964, contained sardonic paragraphs about Hitchcock's later career, and his notions of the therapeutic effect of shocks and suspense. See "The Bald Primaqueera," in *Blasts and Benedictions* (London: Macmillan, 1967), 75-76.

48. Murray deals persuasively with the structure of O'Casey's play (*Sean O'Casey*, 149-50). The importance to Hitchcock of the concept of the "well-made play" is summarized in Barr, *English Hitchcock*, 13.

49. Even in the addendum to his original interview with Truffaut, following *Torn Curtain*, Hitchcock was still keeping this idea in mind: "I'd like to do twenty-four hours in the life of a city, and I can see the whole picture from beginning to end . . ." (Truffaut, *Hitchcock*, 320).

50. Victor Saville, quoted in *Kinematograph Weekly*, 3 October 1929, on his return from Hollywood shortly before Hitchcock started shooting *Juno*. This version of *Woman to Woman* was the sound remake of the film directed by Graham Cutts on which Hitchcock had worked as screenwriter and art director at Islington in 1923 — the first collaboration, for both men, with producer Michael Balcon.

51. A still of Hitchcock behind the bar appears both in *Kinematograph Weekly* (21 November 1929) and *Picturegoer* (January 1930). Unfortunately, no image of a quality suitable for reproduction has been found.

52. McGilligan, *Alfred Hitchcock*, 128.

JOHN HELLMANN

The Birds *and the Kennedy Era*

Critics of *The Birds* (1963) have shown relatively little
interest in the relation of the film to its historical moment.
Instead, they have typically read the film as an existential and
psychological fable. Robin Wood, for instance, finds *The Birds*
a story of human response to catastrophe in which the bird
attacks function as a universal metaphor for the "arbitrary
and unpredictable," while Thomas Leitch perceives the avian
apocalypse to be no more than an absurdist "joke." Others
have sought to establish the birds as allegorical figures for the
emotions or failings apparent in the film's human characters
or in civilization itself: John McCombe sees the birds as
Romantic avengers for "man's alienation from the natural
world"; Margaret Horwitz detects evidence that the birds are
supernatural agents of the mother's jealous emotions blocking
the female protagonist's pursuit of her son; Slavoj Žižek
argues that the bird attacks are more precisely an artistic
cover for a "ferocious female superego"; and both Richard
Allen and Susan Smith make detailed textual analyses
suggesting that the birds are, as Smith puts it, "emotional
sensors, able to detect and express powerful repressed
feelings" of the main adult characters.[1]
   My reading seeks to trace in *The Birds* what Frederic
Jameson calls the "cobwebs of topical allusion" that "texts
send down into the contingent circumstances of their own
historical time."[2] I will demonstrate that *The Birds* includes
specific allusions to slogans, symbols, issues, and events
contemporaneous with its making. *The Birds* is Hitchcock's
sole film produced and released during the brief presidency

of John F. Kennedy, and it affords a refracted view of historical conflict in a distinctly transitional moment.

The certitudes and rigidities of the 1950s did not end in 1960 with JFK's triumphant presidential campaign. Nevertheless, the urgent rhetoric and youthful image of the victorious presidential candidate encouraged rebellious forces to accelerate their demands. As Elaine Tyler May observes, "Shortly after Kennedy's election, the frustrations and resentments that had been expressed in the fifties not only publicly by black civil rights activists, artists, intellectuals, and the 'beats,' but privately by many members of the white middle class, began to surface."[3] Most assertively, the civil rights movement directly confronted discrimination with Freedom Rides, marches, and demonstrations. Many white middle-class women, idealized in the fifties as domestic helpmates and managers, now moved into the public sphere by organizing against the threat of nuclear war. In 1961, under pressure, Kennedy created the President's Commission on the Status of Women, which played a crucial role in articulating the concerns of the nascent women's movement. Students were likewise still expected to follow the dictates of university bureaucracies and the Selective Service draft system. Yet during the campaign JFK had brashly asserted that it was time for "a new generation of leadership," and he called on the nation's youth to give up their comforts for "service." The example of the civil rights movement more particularly helped inspire an era of youthful political radicalism with the founding in 1962 of the Students for a Democratic Society (SDS). In response to the near-catastrophe that same year of the Cuban missile crisis, Bob Dylan composed the apocalyptic "A Hard Rain's A-Gonna Fall," and JFK himself successfully pursued a Nuclear Test Ban treaty, even as his administration continued to prosecute the Cold War in Vietnam and Cuba. The Kennedy era is thus a period of contradiction, in which the social formations of the postwar period were under increasing pressure from forces rebelling against the limits and paradoxes of Cold War policies.

The Birds, in tapping into this specific historical moment, includes elements of both the receding fifties and the emergent sixties, but some of the specific historical material in *The Birds* has faded from the horizon of many of this century's viewers. Even to the original 1963 audience, the subtle topical allusions would have been barely noticed, registered as only passing, insignificant, or irrelevant details. But a sharpened awareness of their significance, one heightened by a retrospective knowledge of events to come, produces meanings and aesthetic effects startlingly different from a reading focused on the cinematic text alone, in the manner of New Criticism, or even one driven by more general cultural perspectives.

In the fantasy-premise of the film, as persuasively demonstrated by Allen and Smith, the bird attacks occur as a symptom formation. Smith traces the evidence in the text that attacks are a manifestation or sign of the "powerful repressed feelings of extreme anger, resentment and fear that ordinarily remain hidden and unacknowledged behind the characters' façades of polite, witty, intellectual conversation and their apparent displays of complacency or indifference."[4] Allen somewhat more specifically states that the bird attacks represent "an uncontrolled rage that issues from feelings of isolation and abandonment."[5] I want to propose that we read those same "feelings" as also necessarily manifestations of Jameson's "political unconscious." History both situates and shapes human characters and their circumstances. From that perspective, the bird attacks become both more specific and richer in significance: they manifest the fears, longings, and frustrations of the period in which the private emotions of the characters necessarily participate.

Bill Krohn has documented that Hitchcock either deleted or severely truncated screenwriter Evan Hunter's most obvious and explicit topical references, even when V.S. Pritchett applauded such attempts to "find parallels for the bird attacks in the world situation."[6] Nevertheless, as we will see, Hitchcock subsequently added the most densely topical, if subtly so, scene of the film. With his characteristic obliqueness, as well as the logic of the horror genre, Hitchcock then pushed the forces alluded to in the topical references toward the apocalyptic disruption of his abstracted, iconic settings of school, town, and home. The memorable images of catastrophe thus encourage us to read back into the film allegorical meanings.

From our present vantage, the Kennedy-era material in *The Birds* cannot be regarded as referring to static, isolated entities frozen in significance with the release of the film, a cinematic correlative to a period memorialized as Camelot, but rather to historical signifiers of forces caught in a dialectical process. *The Birds* can, for that reason, even appear to be an eerie visualization of the longings and anxieties of the period hurtling toward the apocalyptic consequences of the coming years: the collapsing by identity politics of distinct domestic and public spheres; the assaults by activist civil rights and youth movements upon cultural, social, and political hierarchies; and the turning away from patriarchal authority as a source of safety and wisdom. In that sense, as we explore the dimensions of its topical resonance, we may find *The Birds* to be remarkably prescient.

Melanie Daniels on the New Frontier

The opening sequence of *The Birds* suggests a mysterious disturbance of birds circling over society, a specter perhaps focused around a somewhat bird-like figure crossing the street below. The birds gather over Union Square in downtown San Francisco, but this quick-moving, strikingly crested woman is the only person who appears concerned. Furthermore, Melanie Daniels (Tippie Hedren) is headed toward a bird shop. Only after Melanie intrudes into Bodega Bay, with a caged pair of lovebirds in pursuit of Mitch Brenner (Rod Taylor), do the feelings of Melanie and such characters as Annie Hayworth (Suzanne Pleshette) and Lydia Brenner (Jessica Tandy) rise to the level of social chaos manifested by the bird attacks. The domestic melodrama thus seems to be focused on the impact of a restless protagonist upon a tenaciously maintained, but static and unproductive, social formation, and the bird attacks seem to arise as fantastic symptoms of the anxieties and paranoia produced by a threat of change.

If Melanie is the pivotal character in a drama of social conflict, she has a specific topical resonance. Hitchcock's glamorous, young, capable, somewhat madcap, but ultimately earnest heroine exhibits the style and spirit that Jacqueline Kennedy brought to the White House. The deeper connection between Melanie and the Kennedy zeitgeist can be recognized in the scene that provides her backstory. According to Hunter, the credited screenwriter, the scene in which Melanie relates her biography to Mitch as they stand on a sand dune above the birthday party was added at some point after his work on the screenplay was completed. Hitchcock shot the scene over Hunter's objections, and Hunter believed that Hitchcock wrote the scene himself.[7] Its elevated setting, portentously framed by dramatically angled shots of the characters' ascent and descent, suggests that the director wanted to signal an important revelation. Previous critics have properly emphasized the centrality of Melanie's confessions about her mother to a pervasive theme in the film of a fear of abandonment.[8] None, however, has noticed how the scene links that theme to the historical moment.

During his presidential campaign, Kennedy settled upon a rhetorical trope that resonated well with what would become the Kennedy style while responding to the nation's mood. During 1960 the national press published intense exchanges concerning the "national purpose" among cultural spokespersons in what amounted to a national jeremiad. This exhortation was the culmination of doubts that had been expressed throughout the 1950s concerning the effects of postwar affluence and conformity upon the ability of a generation of Americans seen as materialistic and soft to stand up to the challenge of a monolithically dedicated international Communism.[9] In his speech accepting the nomination of the Democratic Party at the 1960 convention in Los Angeles, JFK responded to this anxiety about the

American character. Noting that he was "facing west on what was once the last frontier," he said, "we stand today on the edge of a New Frontier—the frontier of the 1960s, the frontier of unknown opportunities and perils—the frontier of unfulfilled hopes and unfilled threats." He said that beyond that frontier "are uncharted areas of science and space, unsolved problems of peace and war, unconquered pockets of ignorance and prejudice, unanswered questions of poverty and surplus." Arguing that, "courage—not complacency—is our need today," he then urged his national audience to follow him as "new pioneers on that New Frontier."[10]

The New Frontier metaphor offered contemporary citizens an opportunity to see themselves drawing upon a pioneer heritage much celebrated at the time in the Westerns that filled cinema and television screens.[11] After the Democratic convention, Kennedy found campaign audiences responding most strongly to his challenges to service, and in response he strengthened his association of the New Frontier with that theme.[12] Kennedy would insistently repeat this theme during his campaign, culminating in the famous call of his Inaugural Address: "Ask not what your country can do for you; ask what you can do for your country." The New Frontier caught on as the slogan for Kennedy's subsequent administration.

The sand dune scene of *The Birds* duplicates settings associated with Kennedy's New Frontier. Melanie and Mitch's conversation against a backdrop of sea and sand dunes, amid an overlap of the sounds of children playing below and the cries of sea gulls calling overhead, evokes photographs in *Life* and *Look* magazines of the President and his family at the Kennedy compound in Hyannis Port. Those photographs projected the new spirit of adventure, subliminally echoing JFK's legendary World War II service on PT 109 among the Solomon Islands in the Pacific. As in the Kennedy photographs, the inspiring vista of untamed nature implies the presence beyond of distant challenges. The elevation high above the ocean bay carefully sets the testimonial with which Melanie will attempt to prove her worth as a citizen within a visual correlative to the space

Figure 1

of JFK's New Frontier. She speaks to Mitch upon an inspiring and romantic threshold between the domestic, comfortable, familiar world of the backyard birthday party, with its safe children games of family life below, and the dramatic expanse of ocean and blue sky stretching behind and above toward Asia and outer space (fig. 1).

Melanie's dialogue cites Rome, Korea, and Berkeley, major global markers on the postwar American ideological map that possess a moral significance bringing forward the essential terms of a national myth developed in sermons, folklore, slogans, literature, and film over a four-hundred-year-old history of westward expansion. And she describes herself enacting what is recognizably Kennedy's script for national reinvigoration on the New Frontier. The night before, Mitch had offended Melanie by confronting her with a newspaper report that while in Rome the summer before she had jumped "naked" into a public fountain in Rome. Melanie denies that she was nude and claims to have been "pushed into that fountain," but she acknowledges the accuracy of Mitch's accusation that she was running around "with a pretty wild crowd." The report recognizably alludes to Fellini's *La Dolce Vita* (1960), in which a visiting American celebrity played by Anita Ekberg famously wears a low-cut gown as she cavorts in a Roman fountain. In the United States the film was invoked as an icon of an aimlessly hedonistic postwar Europe.

Now, on the sand dune of *The Birds*, Melanie explains, "You see, Rome, that entire summer I did nothing but . . . well, it was very easy to get lost there." While JFK, aided by his French-speaking and Oleg Cassini-dressed First Lady, worked at associating the New Frontier with the attainments of European culture, his rhetoric nevertheless urged Americans to turn away from the temptations of affluence that Americans since Jefferson's sojourn in Paris had feared would lead them into excesses of European sophistication. The New Frontier was an exhortation to embrace only the best of civilization while acting "with vigor" as agents of progress; Americans should revitalize their youthful contrast to a spiritually exhausted Europe by doing good works on the rugged battlefields of the Cold War.

Melanie has clearly caught the spirit of the New Frontier, as she now demonstrates by showing Mitch that she is taken with the prevailing notion that a young woman can serve one's country while still being as stylish as Jackie Kennedy. Declining another refill from Mitch's pitcher of martinis, she proceeds to vindicate her character as a good citizen on the New Frontier before Mitch's skeptical gaze by showing that she is striving to rehabilitate herself from her "lost" condition in Rome: "So when I came back I thought it was time I began, oh, I don't know, finding something again." She details for Mitch her present weekly regimen of philanthropy and intellectual self-improvement, though each assertion of her productive role as citizen elicits from Mitch a skepticism about her character that perhaps also partakes of the patriarchal assumptions of the time regarding the potential of women in the public sphere. In any event, his remarks are each met with a resulting defensive response from Melanie.

For instance, after she announces that on Mondays and Wednesdays she volunteers with Traveler's Aid, Mitch trivializes this "job" by sardonically remarking, "Helping traffic." Melanie evenly replies, "No, misdirecting them—I thought you could read my character." On Thursdays, she defiantly continues, she has her "meeting and lunch," to which Mitch sarcastically appends, "In the underworld, I suppose," thus reminding her, and us, of his assertion during their initial encounter that the judge should have placed her "behind bars." Melanie replies, "I shall disappoint you," and explains that we "actually raise money" to send "a little Korean boy through school," an effort that associates her with the missionary zeal of the Peace Corps, the program JFK initiated to elicit the idealism of American citizens, and which specifically enacts the teacher/student terms of the "nation-building" that was intrinsic to Kennedy's counterinsurgency policies in Third World nations.

Similarly, her announcement that on Tuesdays she attends a course in General Semantics at Berkeley accords with the new prestige of intellectual self-improvement during JFK's administration. A major component of JFK's image was based on his having been awarded the Pulitzer Prize for his book *Profiles in Courage* (1956), and considerable publicity had been accorded JFK's taking a speed-reading course and assembling a cabinet and White House staff consisting of the "best and the brightest" from the nation's elite universities.

Melanie's course in General Semantics has another topical significance as well. While previous commentators on *The Birds* seem to understand Melanie to be studying linguistics, General Semantics was actually a philosophy and training program that had an influence on a number of academic disciplines, but it never established itself in any department in the United States. Centered on the dangers and potential of language in creating an unconscious structuring of "reality" for humans, General Semantics espoused a method for personal and social transformation. A fashionable trend of the late fifties and early sixties, General Semantics was finding its way on the West Coast into therapeutic courses ranging from one with R. Buckminster Fuller for prisoners at San Quentin to a summer seminar-workshop enrolled in by members of industry and even the 1950s television celebrity Steve Allen at the University of California at Santa Barbara. The philosophy was about to have a major influence on science fiction (Frank Herbert, who was at work on the 1966 *Dune*, was like Melanie also taking a General Semantics course at this time in San Francisco).[13] Melanie's enrollment in the course at Berkeley was in the Kennedy spirit, but it also suggests that Hitchcock's protagonist is interested in alternative ways of thinking and living being developed in the California of the early sixties.

Indeed, seeing Mitch's smirk, Melanie abruptly identifies her activity at Berkeley as rebellious, a project of "finding new four-letter words." When a softening Mitch admits that he is very glad that she came into the bird shop, Melanie responds by revealing her errand that day:

> MELANIE: "I have an Aunt Tessa. Do you got an Aunt Tessa?"
> MITCH (shaking his head side to side): "Unh-unh."
> MELANIE: "Well, mine is very prim and straitlaced. I'm giving her a mynah bird when she comes back from Europe. Mynah birds talk, you know. Can you see my Aunt Tessa's face when this one tells us one or two of the words I've picked up at Berkeley?"

Melanie's claim to be "finding new four-letter words" as part of her studies implies that she has been exposed to poetry readings and political dissent at the coffee houses and clubs adjacent to the campus. "Aunt Tessa" is a personification of the pseudo-Victorian mindset of the postwar "containment culture" that had ruled Allen Ginsberg's *Howl* legally obscene, part of a larger social regulation designed to silence any challenge to the social and political order. In 1957 U.S. Customs agents seized copies of *Howl* and arrested Lawrence Ferlinghetti, owner of City Lights bookstore, for trafficking in obscenity. As the beats and political activists gathered on Telegraph Avenue in the late 1950s and early 1960s to form a bohemian community adjacent to the campus, Berkeley shared the notoriety of Ginsberg's poem in becoming a signifier in public consciousness for a use of obscenity as well as leftist agitation that voiced a radical dissent from the political and social taboos constraining Cold War politics and culture. Indeed, Melanie's second reference, "one or two of the words I've picked up at Berkeley," is vague, leaving open the possibility that the words might be any frank expressions of forbidden subjects, from the sexual act to revolution.

With her Aston-Martin DBG sports convertible, her designer outfits and fur coat, and her hair in an elegant French twist, Melanie scarcely appears a member of the bohemian or activist communities. However, in 1962 Helen Gurley Brown's *Sex and the Single Girl* and the film-version of *The Chapman Report* were drawing attention to women's dissatisfaction with prevailing sexual mores; furthermore, concerns about the discontents of educated and financially independent white women had for several years been widely reported, culminating in the publication of Betty Friedan's *The Feminine Mystique* one month before the release of *The Birds*.[14] Melanie's "very prim and straitlaced" Aunt Tessa personifies the repressive pretensions to propriety that worked during the postwar period to contain a variety of forces of dissent and change that the Beats assaulted in part with obscenity, in part with taboo ideas. The uncivil words Melanie plans for the mynah bird to speak to her Aunt Tessa link Melanie's discontents to those of the Beats and political activists. The mynah would relay diverse forces of rebellion gathering momentum during the Kennedy years.

Critics have consistently overlooked this historical reference. Camille Paglia refers to the language Melanie plans to teach the mynah bird as "salty gutter talk," as if Melanie had learned the taboo words from a sailor; in fact, we have seen that Melanie twice emphasizes that she acquired the language at Berkeley.[15] Christopher Morris, like most critics, overlooks Melanie's boast on the sand dune altogether. For Morris, *The Birds* allegorizes Paul de Man's concept of allegory as the figure of the temporal gap between signifier and signified, and thus the impossibility of representation. Because Melanie was told at the bird shop that the mynah had not yet arrived, Morris asserts that "the springboard situation emphasizes the absence of language's referent in its opening narrative of a *missed delivery*." Morris concludes that the significance is precisely that the mynah "has not arrived—the promised 'content' of her language is missing from the beginning."[16] But Morris ignores the scene on the sand dune; as we have seen, the missing "content" of the language that Melanie plans to teach the mynah is in fact revealed in that pivotal scene, and its prohibited status links Melanie's personal rage to a broader historical discontent. Her pranks, of which the mynah-gift to her aunt is planned to follow the sneaking of the caged lovebirds into the Brenner home, are neurotic symptoms that signify the missing language in the story she tells. The mynah will enable Melanie to sit primly before her aunt, outwardly adhering to social regulation even as her other voice speaks her discontents.

The mynah also works as a figure of the film's method of allegory (speaking *allos*, or "other," in the *agora*, the public sphere of the marketplace). In the spectacular bird attacks to follow, the political resonances introduced through Melanie's dialogue from atop the sane dune reverberate in a disruption of school, town, and home. Hitchcock's attention to political content, but artistic determination to convey it only subtly or indirectly, may be inferred from a scene in the screenplay that Hitchcock actually shot but did not include in the film. As she and Mitch jokingly speculate about the cause of the bird attacks, Melanie suggests that they might be led by a Castro-like bird with a little beard, exhorting: "Birds of the world unite! You have nothing to lose but your feathers!"[17] Hitchcock removed this explicit reference to the possibility of a broad political revolt, the dissent stigmatized in the Cold War culture as the threat of the international Communist conspiracy. But he substituted a cloaked reference to such dissent in the scene on the sand dune. Hitchcock structures *The Birds* in an allegorical mode with elements like those Ismail Xavier describes at work in the film *Black God, White Devil* (1964), a "'figural' method" that "transforms history into a referential matrix covered with layers of imaginary constructions."[18] Indeed, the odd aesthetic of *The Birds*, with its long scenes of character-based dialogue or silence, lacking even the emotional rhythm of a musical soundtrack to break the placid surface, abruptly interrupted by fast-paced bird attacks, montages of jump cuts amplified with a jarring electronic soundtrack, suggests the allegorical expression of repressed tensions. We are in a world of outward calm, the world of the Cold War domestic "consensus" and international nuclear stand-off, beneath which rage the forces that increasingly erupted into the crises that characterized the Kennedy years, threatening revolt and destruction.

The Jungle Gym and Telegraph Avenue

Melanie's association of herself with the Beats predictably causes Mitch to reassert his judgment of her as immature: "You need a mother's care, my child." Mitch's statement reminds Melanie of her mother's abandonment, and triggers a furious response: "My mother? Don't waste your time. She ditched us when I was eleven and went off with some hotel man in the East. You know what a mother's love is!" Her momentary breakdown is then followed by a bird attack on the birthday party that begins with a strike at Cathy, who is turning precisely eleven, and then at her mother Lydia, who is bringing out the birthday cake. Melanie's every step toward inserting herself into Bodega Bay produces in both herself and the other adult characters feelings of extreme tension based on underlying rage at the prospect of a change that might bring further abandonment and isolation. These emotions reflect both Melanie's ambivalence about conforming to expectations and the fears of Annie, Lydia, and Mitch that Melanie is a threat to their present social formation. The topical references have served to suggest how these characters' underlying conflicts mirror the broader tensions of the Kennedy era. And those references serve as driving ideas adding meaning to the rather abstract settings for the bird attacks.

Melanie's allegorical spreading of social and political discontent from Berkeley to outwardly placid Bodega Bay attains a visual manifestation in the most iconic scene of *The Birds*, the attack at the Bodega Bay School. The sequence begins as Melanie sits on a bench with her back to the school playground, presenting a *mise-en-scène* in which the parallel shapes of Melanie and a jungle gym tensely balance the composition. The jungle gym duplicates the silhouette of Melanie's shoulder and head, and the two forms lean slightly toward each other. The tightly curved iron railings making up the jungle gym similarly double the patterns of Melanie's tightly bound hair. The fence separating Melanie from the jungle gym behind and to the left side of the screen divides the *mise-en-scène* into a space of Melanie's awareness and a space of her unawareness. Thus the jungle gym, as shadowy doppelgänger and structure for group activity, appears to assert a social possibility that parallels Melanie's unconscious. The simultaneity of Melanie's anxious reaching for a cigarette in her purse with the arrival of the first bird upon the jungle gym suggests that the birds are being "called" by the same thoughts driving her nervous actions. For these reasons, Michael Walker argues that the crows are "being symbolically produced out of her unconscious."[19] This psychological interpretation is compelling, but I want to build on Walker's insight by pointing out that the setting echoes the topical references to another school in Melanie's dialogue on the sand dune.

The specific iconography of school and playground suggests connections between what is taking place on screen and the dissent Melanie cryptically referred to at Berkeley. In that way we can see that the black crows are symptoms of the film's political unconscious. They are symbolically produced out of myriad discontents with which Melanie is allegorically associated. The arrival of the black crows on the "campus" of the Bodega Bay School threatens the orderly singing in unison of the schoolchildren inside the building presided over by the teacher Annie Hayworth, even as the arrival of an activist and bohemian community has threatened the power structure governing the university at Berkeley.

In a film that eschews a conventional soundtrack, the emotions driving Melanie's nervousness are suggested by the words that the children are singing. Melanie has come to the school to fetch Cathy. In the preceding scene in Lydia's bedroom, Melanie initially answered Lydia's worries about Cathy by saying that she was sure her daughter was safe in the care of the schoolteacher Annie. However, Melanie's efforts at reaching out to Lydia during the lengthy exchange of intimate conversation culminated in her offering to go take Cathy away from the school after all. Lydia's grateful thanks indicated that she might stop fearing Melanie as a threat if Melanie is in fact a dutiful, caring prospective daughter-in-law who would not cause Lydia to be "abandoned."

The jungle-gym scene thus comes at a point in the film where Melanie appears to have overcome the last of the three major obstacles to her resolving her own abandonment issues and isolation by entering a home within the traditional social formation represented by Bodega Bay: the skepticism of Mitch regarding her true character, the rivalry of his erstwhile lover and "friend" Annie, and the hostility of his fearful mother Lydia. Yet, as Melanie is on the threshold of a possible marriage to Mitch, a figure of the law and tradition, the song lyrics present a strikingly pessimistic account of the life awaiting a "country wife," and they summarize the gestures that have marked each step of Melanie's conscious moves to that point in the film toward assuming a woman's role in traditional patriarchy.

At Annie's two nights before, Melanie acknowledged that she wanted to "stay," effectively opening herself to marriage with Mitch. Now the schoolchildren sing: "I married my wife in the month of June." As the schoolchildren sing lyrics in which a man narrates the story of his marriage, the lines insistently (and ironically) echo images of Melanie's pursuit of happiness in the form of marriage to a gentleman squire of Bodega Bay. When Melanie thanked Annie for her "permission" to pursue the latter's erstwhile lover, the decision was answered by an ominous thump at the door,

and Melanie pointed out that the dead seagull on the porch
that Annie calls the "poor thing" could not have been lost
in the dark because there is a "full moon." Now the
children sing: "I brought her home by the light of the
moon." After waking up in Mitch's home in an old-
fashioned nightgown purchased at the local general store,
Melanie brushed her loosened hair in a vintage mirror; her
reflected image, the future identity she has been
contemplating, looked back at her from the wall between,
on one side, a pair of framed antique portraits of a genteel
lady and a gentleman, and, on the other, an antique print of
a country squire with his lady. Now the children sing a
cryptic account of the isolation a wife might find under
traditional patriarchy: "She combed her hair but once a
year / With every stroke she shed a tear." Melanie's first
encounter with Mitch climaxed in his use of his hat to
capture a bird she let escape, a bird he then identified as the
Melanie Daniels who needed to be put back in her "gilded
cage," and ended with his tipping his hat to her as he exited
with a smug, "Good day, Miss Daniels." Now, the male
persona, in the song that Melanie listens to, reports that,
when he asked his wife to "wash the floor," she "gave me
my hat and showed me the door." The song articulates a
kind of grim folk wisdom concerning the home Melanie is
pursuing. This story of a marriage comes through the
voices of children, and it perhaps echoes Melanie's
imagination of the state of mind that led her own mother to
run away from her husband and child. The lyrics therefore
plausibly articulate Melanie's own ambivalence, her
underlying fear of the possible consequences of her pursuit
of marriage.

The song lyrics accompany Melanie's apparently inward
gaze. Far from seeming worried about birds, Melanie does
not look upward once until the end of the sequence. Instead,
she looks straight ahead or nervously back in the direction of
the children's singing, her expression growing increasingly
bitter as the words flow out to her (fig. 2a). The visual
montage thus dramatizes darkening thoughts imperceptibly

Figures 2a, 2b, and 2c

multiplying into an unconscious black rage as the birds increasingly mass behind her (figs. 2b and 2c). Referring to Melanie's mottled black outfit in the scene in the bird shop, Richard Allen has pointed out, "It is in retrospect striking

Figure 3. Activist at Berkeley; from *Berkeley in the Sixties*

that Melanie does not wear the costume of a lovebird in this scene but the costume of a death-bird,"[20] an observation strengthened by the fact that the plumage of the bird Melanie had come to purchase, the hill mynah, the variety of mynah bird that can talk, is "jet-black."[21] Viewers might not possess that knowledge, but the fact nevertheless suggests an organizing narrative subtext, an unconscious of the text. The match between the black plumage of the mynah and Melanie's black outfit is a clear parallel to the motif of Melanie's change to a green outfit to carry the green lovebirds. As an unspoken aspect of the off-screen mynah bird, the hidden symbol adds a mysterious weight to the motif of "four-letter words" picked up at Berkeley.

The black crows on the "campus" of the Bodega Bay School will enact in deed the outrage the black-garbed Melanie was planning to "teach" the black mynah to enact in words against the "prim and strait-laced Aunt Tessa." The blackness thus broadens to suggest the political unconscious. If, as Walker suggests, Melanie has somehow unconsciously "called" these death-birds to the Bodega Bay School, she has brought them from the campus of another school. The death-

Figures 4a and 4b

birds are linked to the jet-black mynah, and thus to the activists
and bohemians she listened to on Telegraph Avenue, themselves
gathering at the University of California at Berkeley, threatening
to displace or corrupt the docile students under the tutelage of
their teachers (fig. 3). We might extend the topical associations
further. Activists at Berkeley were both inspired by and
participants in the civil rights movement. And schools, from
Little Rock Central High in 1957 to the University of Mississippi
in 1962, had been major sites of white riot and turmoil as black
Americans, accompanied by federal troops or U.S. marshals,
showed up outside the white-only school buildings.

The scene that follows the jungle-gym sequence, the bird
attack on the schoolchildren as they go down the hill from the
school to the town below (figs. 4a and 4b), can perhaps be

Figure 5. San Francisco City Hall, May 1960;
from *Berkeley in the Sixties*

usefully compared to a much-reported recent event. In May 1960, in what *Newsweek* magazine called an "Un-American 'Quake,' " Berkeley students and area activists gathered at city hall in downtown San Francisco to protest hearings of the House Un-American Activities Committee, a demonstration that culminated in a chaotic melee down the massive front steps into the street below.[22] News footage and photographs in the *San Francisco Chronicle* showed the wild scene as policemen used fire hoses and brute force to send approximately 400 students thumping, tumbling, and sliding down the steps (figs. 5 and 6).[23] Activist and broadcast journalist William Mandel denounced "beaters of children."[24] The experience radicalized many more Berkeley students, leading to further confrontations in downtown San Francisco.

I will not assert that this material is necessarily a specific source for the scene in *The Birds*. I will, however, point out the availability of the material. Hitchcock lived a short distance from San Francisco and "became an active member of the Bay Area by making personal appearances at local universities and enjoying the culture and lifestyle of the region."[25] Moreover,

Figure 6. San Francisco City Hall, May 1960;
from *Berkeley in the Sixties*

the director was always alert to the introduction of chaos into a scene of order, which Spoto calls "perhaps the single most obvious situation in Hitchcock's films."[26] The event occurred little more than a year before Hitchcock and Hunter went to work on the screenplay in September 1961.[27] It is as if Hitchcock maps Telegraph Avenue, the Berkeley campus, and the long steps of San Francisco City Hall upon the playground, Bodega Bay School, and road down to the center of Bodega Bay. Whether or not this particular historical event is a source for Hitchcock's sequence, the bird attacks are likely to be inspired by such scenes of social chaos associated with schools and universities that had been appearing in contemporary newspapers and television reports. In addition, such scenes appeared repeatedly in the waves of films about juvenile delinquency that followed the 1954 novel *Blackboard Jungle,* written by the screenwriter Hitchcock chose for *The Birds.*

My parallel between the crows on the jungle gym with Berkeley activists may seem to be contradicted by my subsequent parallel between the crows and police. But such defiance of surface logic should not dismay us. The Bodega Bay School sequence is obviously surreal, and "discontinuity and unnatural groupings seem to characterize surreal art."[28] The inconsistency and illogic in surrealism follow from a tapping into the deeper logic of Freud's analysis of the mechanisms of the dreamwork. Freud theorized that disparate thoughts fuse, or "condense," through some accidental association possessed by a single image. The image then possesses a disguised force enabling the forbidden ideas to break through the dream "censor" to the manifest dream. Through the oneiric logic of surrealism, both the rebellious Berkeley students and the policemen who pursue them are condensed into harassing crows that send well-behaved schoolchildren running and falling down an incline. The ideas of rebellion and violent repression are linked in the less overt but effectively condensed idea of the chaos resulting from black crows driving children away from school. Hence the black crows constitute a powerfully oblique image. It conveys the threat of social disruption, while evading such censoring mechanisms as the Hollywood Production Code and the desire of Hitchcock to avoid too explicit a parallel with topical events.

A New Generation of Americans

With the New Frontier, JFK configured the uncertainties of a changing world within a nostalgic vision from American myth. Thus the new decade appeared to be an extension of a divinely ordained story rooted in the ideological slogans of Manifest Destiny and Redeemer Nation that had accompanied four-hundred years of westward expansion, with the conclusion implicitly guaranteed if the new generation rose to the challenge.

Hitchcock draws upon the pastoral aspect of the frontier myth in his settings for *The Birds*. Melanie's pursuit of Mitch from San Francisco to Bodega Bay leads from the city to the country. Raymond Williams has observed that one of the reasons "the idea of the country is an idea of childhood" is "the ideally shared communal memory."[29] Upon moving the film out of San Francisco, Hitchcock creates this experience of immersion in nostalgic feelings of childhood and communal memory. The initial scenes of Melanie's entry into Bodega Bay return her to an idealized, older America even as she seems to have returned to the status of a child. Upon Melanie's arrival, the combined postmaster/proprietor of the quaint general store, Mr. Brinkmeyer, dotes on Melanie as if she were a charming, slightly mischievous little girl hoping for a piece of candy. The motif of a magical return to childhood is verbalized when Mr. Brinkmeyer points out the farmhouse across the bay, where he says Lydia Brenner lives with "the two kids—Mitch and the little girl." Thus Melanie, in the pleasing glow of Mr. Brinkmeyer's grandfatherly gaze, hears that the San Francisco lawyer, who in San Francisco scolded her as a kind of overgrown juvenile delinquent, also quaintly regresses to the social identity of a child when he comes home to his rural homestead. The theme of a pleasing move back in time continues when Melanie subsequently learns from Cathy that Mitch retreats to Bodega Bay on weekends to escape a modern urban environment that he likens to "an anthill at the foot of a bridge." In these early scenes Bodega Bay seems for Melanie a nostalgic return to an older, safer America, with the settings drawn to the specifications of the Norman Rockwell paintings that at the time of the film's release appeared in middle-class homes on covers of the *Saturday Evening Post*.

The Brenner house is at the center of this motif. Sitting alone by the bay next to a barn, it appears to be the paradise of a bygone rural America. Historian Daniel Walker Howe identifies the key elements of the family farm that led to its triumph over early-nineteenth-century collectivist experiments as the ideal image of the American way of life:

> The most common and popular utopia of all was simply a family farm. There the average white American could enjoy the dignity of a freehold, exchange help with neighbors during stressful seasons,

entertain the expectation of a good harvest, and hope to
build a competence that would see a couple through
old age with something to pass on to their children. By
comparison with what was available in Europe, such a
place indeed seemed God's promised land.[30]

In the early 1960s this ideal was celebrated in the popular
westerns of television and movies. Even as the reality of the
family farm was receding, Americans cultivated the dream in
their postwar move to the suburbs. Hitchcock carefully draws
the Brenner family farm to the nostalgic shape of the family farm,
but the rather anonymous interior decor suggests that it is really
the typical American suburban family home of the early 1960s.

This motif provides Mitch Brenner the opportunity in the
final scene of the film to defend the ideal American way of
life. As the masculine head of household, he desperately
fights a siege of birds upon the nuclear family. Mitch's efforts
seem to evoke those of the colonial-era and nineteenth-
century yeoman farmer against Indian marauders, even as the
inevitable futility of those efforts resonates with the plight of
the Kennedy-era suburban male imagining how to protect his
family in the event of nuclear war.

The scene in which Mitch must confront the likelihood of
a bird attack upon the Brenner home includes a topical
reference to JFK's response to the escalating nuclear tensions.
Patrick McGilligan claims that, in following his "instincts,"
Hitchcock deleted Hunter's Cold War references from the
screenplay, even when Pritchett urged keeping them:

> For example, Pritchett praised the scene where
> President Kennedy's State of the Union Address is
> overheard on the radio as Mitch is boarding up the
> Brenner house for the climactic bird attack. In the
> speech, Kennedy extols America's role as "the great
> defender of freedom in its hour of maximum
> danger." Although Pritchett appreciated the Cold
> War irony of this passage, Hitchcock eliminated it
> during the final editing.[31]

Figure 7

In fact, Hitchcock did not eliminate the use of JFK's speech. He instead substituted President Kennedy's words leading up to the phrase in Hunter's screenplay, moved the material to the subsequent scene, and placed them in the voice of a radio announcer who is reporting the President's State of the Union Address. With this revision, Hitchcock made subtler use of the topical reference. But Hitchcock's revision also makes the JFK allusion more effective. The substituted and repositioned phrase helps to unify the film in two ways. The JFK quotation in *The Birds* refers the film back to Melanie's implicit claims on the sand dune to have responded to JFK's New Frontier challenge to Americans, and it brings the New Frontier theme "home" to the "family romance" of the domestic melodrama involving Mitch, Lydia, Melanie, and the dead patriarch Frank Brenner.

On screen, in the scene in which Mitch is on a ladder boarding up an upstairs window, the Kennedy words from Hunter's screenplay about defending freedom are indeed nowhere to be heard. Instead, we watch Mitch's preparations for home defense as he calls Melanie "darling," as if she were already his wife. Indeed, she serves as his suburban helpmate, or a pioneer wife, handing up a board (fig. 7). She also tells him that she cannot reach her father because the line is "dead." The significance of this dialogue contains a parallel to the Kennedy rhetoric and symbolism, and specifically to the JFK quote that Hitchcock will employ in the next scene. Mitch and Melanie are now a couple on their own, like the valiant young couple modeled for their generation by Jack and Jackie Kennedy. They cannot rely on help from a benign patriarch, not Melanie's wealthy and powerful father, and not the father-figure who protected the complacent fifties, President Dwight Eisenhower, with his authority solidly based on his knowledge and experience during World War II as the victorious Supreme Commander of the Allied Armies in Europe.

This generational significance is emphasized when the young couple come back inside the house. Mitch's inability to answer Lydia's anxious questions about where they will go elicits her furious outburst: "You don't know, you don't know, I wish your father were here!" Both Lydia and Mitch are clearly appalled by this revelation of Lydia's lack of faith in Mitch's masculine assurance, and Lydia contritely apologizes. Hitchcock then uses the soundtrack to add the topical resonance. As the humiliated Mitch suggests they all stay calm, we can hear in the background the announcer on the radio saying something about "Europe" and "security," a clear reference to the Cold War tensions over Berlin that had led President Kennedy to urge Americans to consider building nuclear fallout shelters in their homes, a statement that had intensified fears of imminent nuclear war and led many to doubt the young President's wisdom.

It is at this point that Hitchcock places his strategically chosen Kennedy quotation. Mitch turns to Melanie, and they begin walking away together from Lydia toward the outside door. In the background, the announcer on the radio station can then be heard reporting JFK's 1962 speech on the State of the Union, in which the young president quoted his own Inaugural Address. As the young couple go outside onto the porch, the following words are clearly audible: "The president said, 'When I assumed this post a year ago, I said that few generations . . . .'" The rest of the words could easily be filled in by an audience familiar with JFK's

Figure 8

martial vision of the 1960s as an opportunity for a new generation to prove their worthiness: ". . . have been granted the role of defending freedom in its time of maximum danger." Indeed, some might well recall the next lines that the eager young JFK stated in the Inaugural Address that he is here quoting in his State of the Union: "I do not shrink from this responsibility—I welcome it." The emphasis of the words actually quoted adds meaning to the personal stakes for the "new generation," the young couple Mitch and Melanie, as they walk away from Lydia's stated lack of faith in Mitch's masculine adequacy. They go out alone onto the porch.

Once outside, they discuss the uncertain future while watching a flock of birds flying inland, perhaps toward Santa Rosa. The State of the Union Address places the film in January 1962, but Hitchcock certainly knew that the audience of his film would identify Melanie and Mitch's fearful gaze upward with their own watching of the skies during the Cuban missile crisis (fig. 8). For a week during the following October, the world watched in suspense as the confrontation between JFK and Soviet Premier Khrushchev threatened to engulf everyone in nuclear destruction. As Mitch prepares for the inevitable attack by the birds, Hitchcock shapes the Brenner homestead according to the Kennedy-era nightmare of huddling in a suburban basement or backyard nuclear fallout shelter. But he also visually dramatizes, however ironically, the New Frontier idea that this situation is somehow like that of the pioneer forebears.

Raymond Durgnat is very helpful here, as he describes "the extent to which the Brenners' rich home becomes a log cabin, battened down, as the beak-tomahawks break in through the roof or peck away at the heavy mahogany-backed mirror stand, until, eventually, some biological bugle blows, and the God of Nature cries, 'enough—they have held out—I recognize them as mine—they deserve to survive.' "[32] As Durgnat indicates, the Brenners seem less a small town family than contemporary urbanites living in the comfortable setting of a rural homestead. They are thus idealized suburbanites, embattled by symbolic Indians, and they will at last be saved by the "biological bugle" of a symbolic U.S. cavalry sent by the ideological imperatives constraining the possibilities of the film's narrative. In terms of the topical resonance, they are the nuclear family, who, when they face the Cold War nightmare of destruction, face it with the mythic assurances of JFK's "defenders of freedom" on the New Frontier.

Yet Hitchcock ultimately offers considerably less assurance than either Durgnat or JFK. During the preceding attack on the town, Melanie does seem to be ultimately protected by a mediation of the horror she witnesses. When she runs into a telephone booth for shelter, she views actual catastrophes, the "news," unfolding on the viewing "screens" formed by the transparent glass panels. Melanie watches out-of-control fire hoses and tumbling firemen fill the screen in a spectacularly amplified slapstick comedy sketch reminiscent of *The Red Skelton Show*. In a historical anachronism that amused the actual inhabitants of Bodega Bay, she sees a horse-drawn outboard wagon stampede around the corner as if she is watching an episode of the Western, *Gunsmoke*;[33] the ghastly face of a man attacked by birds staggers into "close-up" seemingly from the horror series *Twilight Zone*. This montage resembles an out-of-control changing of channels, duplicating Americans' mediated experience during the Cuban missile crisis, a news spectacle that threatened to overwhelm the soothing forms of conventional television entertainment as well as of JFK's New Frontier myth. In further point-of-view shots, birds begin diving straight at Melanie, and ostensibly the viewer of the film, hitting the "screens" separating the spectator from the spectacle, shattering the plate-glass panels into fragmented patterns as Melanie recoils. Hitchcock thus dramatizes the intense anxiety that can ultimately threaten the "safe" viewer. But, as in a dream or a Western, the seemingly inevitable death does not happen, for the masculine hero Mitch rescues the helpless Melanie just before the horror on the other side of the screen can break through.

Yet a "hole" between screen and reality subsequently appears in the form of an opening in an attic room of the Brenner home. Melanie enters to find herself enclosed with birds. Thus the world of *The Birds* proves finally less safe than the mediated experience of television, American cultural mythology, and Durgnat's account of Hitchcock's film. Ravaged by birds, Melanie is only rescued by Mitch after we have experienced with her an excruciating repeat of the telephone booth scene, this time without intervening "screens," and after our identification-figure has been reduced to a catatonic state. The film switches its focus to Mitch, as the head of the household must prepare an escape from the Brenner homestead for San Francisco. With Melanie placed in the back seat of her car in the arms of Lydia, while Cathy holds the caged lovebirds in the seat next to Mitch, this confused configuration of the postwar American family flees the traditional farmhouse for the hospital in the city, accelerating in a contemporary foreign sports car, an image presenting the contending forces just under the surface during the Kennedy years.

An Apocalyptic Logic

For the most part, in her evocative British Film Institute book on *The Birds*, Camille Paglia follows the lead of previous criticism on the film, inflected by her own interest in sexual personae, as she depicts Hitchcock's film as a work about the timeless and universal conflict between civilization and nature, particularly as manifested through "woman's sexual glamour."[34] However, she pauses at one point to propose a more historically specific, if uncannily anachronistic, set of referents for the sensational bird attacks:

> In retrospect, these images have gained prophetic power about the 60s: Hitchcock seems to have anticipated that decade's thrill killings and political assassinations, with their fatal head wounds, as well as the senseless looting and riots. And the Dionysian excesses of psychedelia too: Dan Fawcett's dead eyes, with their tracks of bloody tears, look like those of the drugged Beatles staring into the void in Richard Avedon's classic Day-Glo icons for *Life* magazine.[35]

From our retrospective vantage, the sensational bird attacks can indeed now seem to elicit a weird *déjà vu* in regard to the tumultuous ten years that followed its March 1963 release.

I would suggest, however, that *The Birds* may now seem to prophesy the subsequent apocalyptic events of the sixties because Hitchcock and his collaborators picked up issues and symbols of their own time, the Kennedy era, and spun them with the apocalyptic logic of the horror genre. Historians have placed those same Kennedy-era symbols and issues at the genesis of the allegorical narrative by which we have interpreted the explosive events that subsequently punctuated the '60s. We call that allegory history. Perceiving our present allegorical understanding of the subsequent events of that decade reflected to us from Hitchcock's 1963 film produces the effect of biblical typology, in which later interpreters see in a text its "prophetic power." In our more modest act of historicist criticism, we have at least glimpsed the process by which the real surged from the repressed discontents and discourses of the Kennedy era into the designs of Hitchcock's apocalyptic film, before those same forces erupted into the apocalyptic sixties.

Acknowledgments

This article is an expanded and revised version of a paper I presented at the Ohio State University, "The Prophetic Power of *The Birds*," at a forum sponsored by Project Narrative on March 31, 2009. I would very much like to thank James Phelan for that opportunity, Ron Green for moderating the event, and Linda Mizejewski for serving as respondent. One of the pleasures of developing this essay has been the benefit of constructive suggestions from colleagues who responded to my ideas in various drafts. In addition to those named above, I would like to thank Nancy Stewart, who served as my Graduate Research Assistant during spring 2009, David Herman, Brian McHale, James Machor, David Adams, John Carlos Rowe, Sidney Gottlieb, and Richard Allen.

Notes

1. Robin Wood, *Hitchcock's Films Revisited* (New York: Columbia University Press, 1989), 154; Thomas M. Leitch, *Find the Director and Other Hitchcock Games* (Athens: University of Georgia Press, 1991), 229; John P. McCombe, " 'Oh, I See . . .': *The Birds* and the Culmination of Hitchcock's Hyper-Romantic Vision," *Cinema Journal* 44 (spring 2005), 78; Margaret M. Horwitz, "*The Birds*: A Mother's Love," in *A Hitchcock Reader*, ed. Marshall Deutelbaum and Leland Poague (Ames: Iowa State University, 1986), 281; Slavoj Žižek, "The Hitchcockian Blot," in *Alfred Hitchcock: Centenary Essays*, ed. Richard Allen and Sam Ishii-Gonzáles (London: BFI, 1999), 132; Richard Allen, "Avian Metaphor in *The Birds*," *Hitchcock Annual* (1997-98), 42-43; Susan Smith, *Hitchcock: Suspense, Humour and Tone* (London: British Film Institute, 2000), 133.

2. Frederic Jameson, *The Political Unconscious: Narrative as a Socially Symbolic Act* (Ithaca, New York: Cornell University Press, 1981), 34.

3. Elaine Tyler May, *Homeward Bound: American Families in the Cold War Era*, rev. ed. (New York: Basic Books, 2008), 208.

4. Smith, *Hitchcock: Suspense, Humour and Tone*, 133.

5. Allen, "Avian Metaphor in *The Birds*," 43.

6. Bill Krohn, *Hitchcock at Work* (London: Phaidon Press, 2000), 247.

7. Evan Hunter, *Me and Hitch* (London: Faber and Faber, 1997), 70.

8. Donald Spoto, *The Dark Side of Genius: The Life of Alfred Hitchcock* (New York: Little, Brown, 1983), 489-90; Allen, "Avian

Metaphor in *The Birds*," 43-45; Smith, *Hitchcock: Suspense, Humour and Tone*, 137.

9. John W. Jeffries, "The 'Quest for the National Purpose' of 1960," *American Quarterly* (1978) 30: 451-70; Eric F. Goldman, *The Crucial Decade and After: America, 1945-1960* (New York: Random House, 1960), 342-43.

10. "Texts of Kennedy and Johnson Speeches Accepting Democratic Nominations," *New York Times*, 16 July 1960.

11. Richard Slotkin, *Gunfighter Nation: The Myth of the Frontier in Twentieth-Century America* (New York: Atheneum, 1992), 379-404.

12. John Hellmann, *The Kennedy Obsession: The American Myth of JFK* (New York: Columbia University Press, 1997), 125.

13. See "The Institute of General Semantics 1961 Summer Seminar-Workshop," The Institute of General Semantics, at http://www.generalsemantics.org/our-offerings/programming-classes/classes-seminars/the-institute-of-general-semantics-1961-summer-seminar-workshop/, accessed August 14, 2011; "Buckminster Fuller: San Quentin Prison, 31 Jan. 1959," *YouTube*, accessed August 2, 2011; Timothy O'Reilly, *Frank Herbert* (New York: Frederick Ungar, 1981), 59-60.

14. James T. Patterson, *Grand Expectations: The United States, 1945-1974* (New York: Oxford University Press, 1996), 448; Daniel Horowitz, *Betty Friedan and the Making of the Feminine Mystique: The American Left, the Cold War, and Modern Feminism* (Amherst: University of Massachusetts Press, 1998), 201-02.

15. Camille Paglia, *The Birds* (London: British Film Institute, 1998), 23.

16. Christopher Morris, "Reading the Birds and *The Birds*," *Literature Film Quarterly*, 28 (2000), 254.

17. Krohn, *Hitchcock at Work*, 248.

18. Ismail Xavier, "*Black God, White Devil*: The Representation of History," in *The Historical Film: History and Memory in Media*, ed. Marcia Landy (New Brunswick: Rutgers University Press, 2001), 253.

19. Michael Walker, *Hitchcock's Motifs* (Amsterdam: Amsterdam University Press, 2005), 109.

20. Allen, "Avian Metaphor in *The Birds*," 54.

21. Sálim Ali and S. Dillon Ripley, *Larks to the Grey Hypocolius* (Bombay: Oxford University Press, 1972), vol. 5 of *Handbook of the Birds of India and Pakistan*, 191.

22. Donald E. Phillips, *Student Protest, 1960-1969: An Analysis of the Issues and Speeches* (Washington, DC: University Press of America,

1980), 24; *Berkeley in the Sixties*, director Mark Kitchell (First Run Features, 1990), DVD; *Through Our Eyes: The 20th-Century As Seen by the San Francisco Chronicle* (San Francisco: Chronicle, 1987), 63.

23. "Arrests at HUAC in City Hall," Moving Image Archive: Shaping San Francisco, at http://www.archive.org/details/ ssfHUAC4, accessed August 14, 2011.

24. "Mandel at HUAC in City Hall 1960," Moving Image Archive: Shaping San Francisco, at http://www.archive.org/details/ MANDEL, accessed August 14, 2011.

25. Jeff Kraft and Aaron Leventhal, *Footsteps in the Fog: Alfred Hitchcock's San Francisco* (Santa Monica: Santa Monica Press, 2002), 261.

26. Spoto, *The Dark Side of Genius*, 39.

27. Hunter, *Me and Hitch*, 11.

28. Angus Fletcher, *Allegory: Theory of a Symbolic Mode* (Ithaca: Cornell University Press, 1964), 379.

29. Raymond Williams, *The Country and the City* (New York: Oxford University Press, 1973), 297.

30. Daniel Walker Howe, *What God Hath Wrought: The Transformation of America, 1815-1848* (Oxford: Oxford University Press, 2007), 303.

31. Patrick McGilligan, *Alfred Hitchcock: A Life in Darkness and Light* (New York: ReganBooks, 2003), 624.

32. Raymond Durgnat, *The Strange Case of Alfred Hitchcock, or the Plain Man's Hitchcock* (Cambridge: MIT Press, 1978), 340.

33. Kraft and Leventhal, *Footsteps in the Fog*, 218.

34. Paglia, *The Birds*, 7.

35. Paglia, *The Birds*, 64.

ERIKA BALSOM

Dial "M" for Museum:
The Hitchcock of Contemporary Art

Since the early 1990s, contemporary artists have engaged in something of an obsession with cinema. Though artists have used film and video for decades, they have most often asserted a certain distance between their employments of these media and the cinema proper, aligning their work instead with other areas of practice, such as performance or sculpture. Due to its status as an illusionistic medium of mass entertainment, cinema itself was a "bad object" to be refused, or at the very least dismantled. All of this changes in the 1990s, when, amidst technological innovations like data projection and the commercialization of the Internet, cinema is reconceived as an immense resource of images, forms, and techniques to be reworked and remade within the spaces of art. One sees a spate of cinema-themed exhibitions, a renewed used of 16mm film, a rehabilitation of fiction and documentary (formerly anathema in artists' film and video), and spectacular projected-image installations with budgets comparable to those of independent feature films.

In this flurry of cinematic art practices, one strand of aesthetic production has asserted itself as especially prominent: the remake of an existing film, most often a Hollywood film. Artists have made much use of the new malleability of cinema after digitization to produce a corpus of found-footage work that—very much unlike many of the films produced in that vein before the 1990s—absolutely depends on the spectator's familiarity with the source material.[1] The remake also extends beyond recycling: films have been reenacted and translated into other media. While these films and videos cite numerous filmmakers from Hollywood and beyond, none appears more frequently than a director who was himself fascinated by fine art, Alfred Hitchcock. In museums and galleries around the world, his films have been slowed down, speeded up, reenacted, and recut. Sets have been reconstructed, shooting locations have been visited, and letters have been written to his characters. Art institutions have followed artists' interest in the director: Hitchcock was the most represented filmmaker in *Hall of Mirrors: Art and Film Since 1945* (Museum of Contemporary Art, Los Angeles, 1996) and the Hayward Gallery, London, named their exhibition *Spellbound: Art and Film* (1996) after his 1945 film. In 1999, the exhibition *Notorious: Hitchcock and Contemporary Art* (Museum of Modern Art, Oxford) was entirely dedicated to taking stock of contemporary artists engaging with Hitchcock, while *Obsessionen: Die Alptraum-Fabrik des Alfred Hitchcock* (Filmmuseum Düsseldorf) also celebrated the centennial of the director's birth but concentrated on film clips and memorabilia. In 2001, *Hitchcock et l'art: coïncidences fatales* (Centre Pompidou, Paris, and Musée d'art moderne, Montreal) explored the correspondences between the filmmaker and visual art of the nineteenth and twentieth centuries.[2] Hitchcock is a director who has many faces, one who has been ceaselessly reinvented by critics and filmmakers alike.[3] But as these examples suggest, over the past two decades yet another "Hitchcock" has emerged: the Hitchcock of contemporary art.

*   *   *   *   *

The earliest invocations of Hitchcock in art appear in still photography. Cindy Sherman's *Untitled Film Stills* (1978-1980) make no specific reference to the director, favoring the appropriation of cinematic codes rather than the citation of specific films, but they do employ some of his signature tropes and constitute a key moment in art's turn towards cinema. Victor Burgin's photograph-and-text piece *The Bridge* (1984) brings together John Everett Millais's *Ophelia* (1851-52) with Madeleine Elster's attempted suicide in *Vertigo* to comment on the gendered gaze. In *Ask The Dusk: North by Northwest* (1959/1990) and *Ask the Dusk: Vertigo* (1958/1990), Cindy Bernard reconstructs landscape shots from the titular films and photographs them in the same aspect ratio as the original using information supplied by personnel who worked on the film to attain the proper effect. Moving away from still photography, Christian Marclay's *Vertigo (Soundtrack to an Exhibition)* (1990) re-edits the soundtrack of this tale of time-sickness so as to trigger a jumble of disjointed memories in the gallery visitor.

Stan Douglas's *Subject to a Film: Marnie* (1989) marks the first time that a Hitchcock film was remade using moving-image media in an art context. This six-minute black-and-white 16mm film is a reenactment of the robbery sequence from *Marnie* (1964) set in the present day. At the moment when the title character's hands are on the safe, the film loops back to the beginning, resulting in a crime forever in process and never discovered. Due to this circularity, Marnie is imprisoned in an eternal return of never-ending theft but given salvation from another kind of imprisonment: marrying Mark Rutland. *Subject to a Film: Marnie* initiates an interest in filmic reenactments that would continue throughout the 1990s. In 1995, Pierre Huyghe reshot the entirety of *Rear Window* (1954) and titled the result *Remake*. Hitchcock appears repeatedly in Brice Dellsperger's *Body Double* series (1995-present), both via Brian De Palma in reenactments of Hitchcockian moments in *Body Double* (1984) as *Body Double #3* (1995), *Dressed to Kill* (1980) as *Body Double #5* (1996), and *Obsession* (1976) as *Body Double #10* and *Body Double #11* (both 1997), and straight up in *Body Double #4* (1996), in which a drag queen reenacts Marion Crane's drive to the Bates motel, complete with a disco soundtrack to erase the voiceover echoes of her guilty conscience. As Richard Allen notes, Gus Van Sant's 1998 shot-by-shot remake of *Psycho* had no precedent in the history of film, but it certainly did have multiple precedents within the history of art.[4]

Figure 1. Christopher Draeger, still from
Schizo (Redux) (2004). Courtesy of the artist.

Douglas Gordon's *24 Hour Psycho* (1993) is perhaps
contemporary art's most famous appropriation of Hitchcock
or, for that matter, of Hollywood cinema in general. As its title
suggests, the installation recycles *Psycho*, slowing it to last
twenty-four hours. Gordon used a commercially available
VHS tape and a Panasonic VCR capable of playing at a speed
of roughly two frames per second to achieve the desired
effect.[5] The resulting images are projected without sound on a
translucent screen hanging in the middle of the gallery. The
installation takes the dilation of time that is central to filmic
suspense and hyperbolizes it so as to defeat suspense entirely.
The private cinema of the VHS tape—with its domestic setting
and increased playback control—is here rendered gigantic
and transported into the public sphere. *24 Hour Psycho* is but
one of many works Gordon has made involving Hitchcock:
Feature Film (1999) isolates the soundtrack of *Vertigo* and
uses extreme close-ups to depict James Conlon conducting
Bernard Hermann's score on a large screen while the
original plays silently on a small monitor; *Empire* (1998)
reproduces the neon hotel sign from *Vertigo* on a Glasgow

Figure 2. Christopher Draeger, still from
Schizo (Redux) (2004). Courtesy of the artist.

street; *A Souvenir of Non-Existence* (1993) mimics the actions of
L.B. "Jeff" Jefferies in *Rear Window* by sending a letter to Lars
Thorwald reading "What have you done with her?" only to
have it returned by the postal service.[6]

It is, however, the rigor mortis of Gordon's daylong "time
readymade," as Hans-Ulrich Obrist describes the approach,
that has proved most influential.[7] In the years that followed the
appearance of *24 Hour Psycho*, many other artists have pursued
Gordon's interest in recycling Hitchcock, some following his
lead of altering the footage simply but significantly, and others
opting to drastically rework it. In the former vein, Christoph
Draeger's *Schizo (Redux)* (2004) superimposes Gus Van Sant's
Psycho over the original in a ghostly doubling. What had
supposedly been an exact copy is revealed as anything but, as
Van Sant's version regularly makes use of closer shot scales
than Hitchcock's. The heads of Anne Heche and Vince
Vaughn appear as inflated semi-transparencies hovering over
those of Janet Leigh and Anthony Perkins, who recede into
the background (figs. 1 and 2). Martijn Hendriks's *Untitled
(Give Us Today Our Daily Terror)* (2008) is a full-length copy of

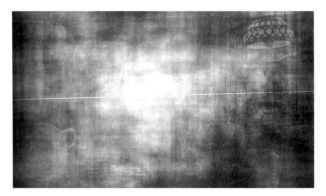

Figure 3. Jim Campbell, *Illuminated Average #1:
Hitchcock's Psycho* (2000). Courtesy of the artist.

The Birds (1963) from which all the birds have been
removed. *Vertigo* is one of seven films included in *Respect
the Dead* (2001-09), a work in which Pierre Bismuth reedits
films to jump to their closing credits immediately
following their first death (in the case of *Vertigo*, that of
Scottie's partner).[8]

Other artists more actively carve up Hitchcock's films:
Christoph Girardet and Matthias Müller's *The Phoenix Tapes*
(1999) is a forty-five-minute video in six parts made entirely
of found footage from forty Hitchcock films, while Les
LeVeque's *2 Spellbound* (1999) and *4 Vertigo* (2000) offer
kaleidoscopic condensations of their title films.[9] In Jim
Campbell's *Illuminated Average #1: Hitchcock's Psycho* (2000),
the artist scanned every frame of the film into a computer and
then superimposed them on top of one another to produce a
single image, displayed in a light box. The center of the frame
becomes a washed-out blur, with only the slightest trace of a
parlor lamp visible in the upper right-hand corner (fig. 3).
Campbell's *Accumulating Psycho* (2004) is a video that shows
this process in action, with *Psycho*'s digitized frames piling up
on top of one another until the film ends with the image of
Illuminated Average #1.[10]

Though re-enactment and recycling constitute the most
popular ways of remaking Hitchcock, there are other ways of

Figure 4. Daniel Pitín, *Birds* (2004). Courtesy of
the artist and Hunt Kastner Artworks.

engaging with the director. For *Scottie's Bedroom* and *Judy's Bedroom* (both 1994), David Reed recreated these *Vertigo* sets, displaying his own paintings over the beds and digitally inserting them into a video of the film playing in the corner of the installation. In 2004, Daniel Pitín produced a series of oil paintings based on stills from *The Birds*. The titular figures appear nowhere in the painting reproduced here (fig. 4), but instead find their disruptive force metaphorized as a painterly smear that troubles representational coherence. For *Self-Portrait as a Fountain* (2000), Paul Pfeiffer made a reproduction of the set of the shower scene from *Psycho*. Chris Marker's 1997 CD-ROM *Immemory* prominently features Hitchcock in its "memory zone" as one of the two paths (the other being Proust) that may be taken by the user to investigate the question "What is a Madeleine?" Daniel Canogar's *Dial "M" For Murder* (2009) is a cat's cradle-like structure constructed from tape unspooled from a VHS copy

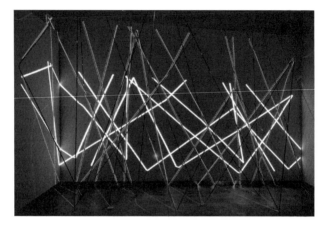

Figure 5. Daniel Canogar, *Dial "M" for Murder* (2010).
Courtesy of Bitforms Gallery.

of Hitchcock's film with a video projected onto it that mimics the scanning motion of the VCR head (fig. 5). Whatever the method employed to rework the director's films, it is undeniable that Hitchcock figures as something of an obsession for artists in the 1990s and 2000s.

As the frenzy of Hitchcock remakes entered its second decade, works begin to appear that function as meta-commentaries on the phenomenon while continuing to participate in it. In appropriating Van Sant's infamous shot-by-shot remake of *Psycho* as raw material, Draeger's *Schizo (Redux)* activates a self-consciousness about the very strategy with which he and so many of his contemporaries are engaged: he produces not simply a remake, but a remake about the proliferation of remakes. Gordon himself returned to *24 Hour Psycho* in 2008, remaking his remake as *24 hour psycho back and forth and to and fro*, a double screen projection that plays the slowed down film forward on one screen and backward on the other. In *Looking for Alfred* (2005) and *Double Take* (2009), Johan Grimonprez abandons the possibility of remaking Hitchcock's films to instead explore the remaking of Hitchcock himself, his shifting identities and carefully cultivated self-presentations. Through this perhaps unlikely avenue, Grimonprez obliquely approaches the question of why precisely Hitchcock might exert such a fascination over contemporary artists and audiences. *Looking for Alfred*, a ten-minute video of Hitchcock impersonators inhabiting the Palais des Beaux Arts in Brussels, is something of a preparatory sketch for *Double Take*, a feature-length collage work that ransacks the audio-visual archive. Embracing a style that one critic has called "post-Internet" with "nods to YouTube," *Double Take*—which will be discussed at greater length in the pages that follow—searches for possible premonitions of and explanations for the proliferation of "Hitchcocks" one encounters today across a diverse collection of fictions, documents, and images.[11]

Grimonprez participates in contemporary art's obsession with Hitchcock and also interrogates its possible roots. He raises crucial questions: Given the virtual obsession with remaking film history in contemporary art, why exactly is it that Hitchcock appears more than any other filmmaker? How can one account for the immense appeal the director has had for a generation of artists born in the early-to-mid-1960s?[12] And what can this tell us about the nature of contemporary art's more general obsession with remaking cinema? The following pages will offer several hypotheses on this front and, in doing so, will outline the characteristics that one might ascribe to the Hitchcock of contemporary art.

*   *   *   *   *

In *Le temps exposé: Le cinéma de la salle au musée*, Dominique Païni writes that Hitchcock was "the filmmaker who reflected more than others, *through his films*, on the intersection of cinema and art history," a statement which begins to hint at the appeal the director might have for contemporary artists and curators.[13] Hitchcock's interest in art and his conception of the image as a plastic surface make him amenable to a gallery context. Through this reframing of his work, intersections between the histories of cinema and art might emerge—something that Païni explored in his *Hitchcock et l'art: coïncidence fatales* exhibition. But there is surely more to it than this: Hitchcock has, after all, been the subject of remaking before, whether by critics or by filmmakers such as Claude Chabrol, Brian De Palma, Chris Marker, François Truffaut, and Gus Van Sant.[14] It is almost as if Hitchcock compels an obsessive rethinking and replaying of his *oeuvre* in those who encounter it. For many of these filmmakers, the project of negotiating Hitchcock's enduring influence has been closely intertwined with the desire to contribute to his critical reception. Though contemporary artists are encountering Hitchcock from a remove, from the sphere of art, where his influence does not loom large as it does in the cinema, they share with filmmakers like Truffaut and De Palma an interest in engaging in a kind of meta-critique of the manifold ways in which Hitchcock's work has been discussed and disseminated. For artists interested in mobilizing the remake as a strategy tied to a critique of originality and an interest in the afterlife of media images, remaking a director who has been remade so many times before might be of special appeal. Rather than entering into a binary relationship between original and copy, the artist instead intervenes in a series of interlocking representations detached from a stable point of origin. The artist remakes Hitchcock, but in doing so also engages with the ways in which the director's films have circulated diffusely throughout popular culture. One has the sense that the more often Hitchcock is remade, the more suitable he is in the eyes of contemporary artists for remaking.

The abundance of Hitchcock remakes in art and film alike leads to another hypothesis: there is something in the films themselves, in their thematic concerns and methods of formal organization, that can account for artists' attraction to the director and the suitability of his films for remaking. Hitchcock's special affinity for art certainly contributes to the way in which he has been embraced within a gallery context.[15] But there is also a preoccupation, within his cinema, with tropes central to the remake itself—namely, the double and the fetish. Perhaps it is the sheer prevalence of these tropes that has prompted filmmakers and artists alike to remake—to double and fetishize, that is—Hitchcock's films over and over again. Examining how these tropes surface in artists' remakes of Hitchcock will sketch some preliminary characteristics of the Hitchcock of

Figure 6. Les LeVeque, still from
2 *Spellbound* (1999). Courtesy of the artist.

contemporary art and provide a much needed opportunity to take account of what kinds of relationships these kleptomaniac artworks set up to the films they appropriate.

*   *   *   *   *

The double is a trope that is closely linked to the cinema itself, that apparatus of mechanical reproduction that disseminates copies of physical reality. A true inheritor of Expressionism, Hitchcock's cinema abounds with doubles. One might think of the case of a falsely accused man mistaken for another (*Frenzy* [1972], *The Lodger* [1927], *North by Northwest* [1959], *The Wrong Man* [1956]), the Madeleine/Judy pair of *Vertigo*, the structural conceit of having the courtyard across from Jeff in *Rear Window* function as a dream-screen that exaggeratedly mirrors aspects of his own psychic life, or any number of other examples. And what is the remake if not a form of doubling, an uncanny return of the familiar made strange? The remakes of Hitchcock in contemporary art draw upon the prevalence of doubles in his films to generate strategies for aesthetic production. In LeVeque's 2 *Spellbound* (fig. 6) and 4 *Vertigo*, for example, images from films dealing with multiple and conflicted identities are themselves multiplied and obscured, manipulated so as to formally manifest the thematic concerns of the title films. In *2 Spellbound*, LeVeque samples frames from the title film and reverses every other frame along the vertical axis to produce a mirrored Rorschach blot-like video lasting only seven-and-a-half minutes.

But unlike Hitchcock's films, in which the double must be vanquished—Michael Walker has suggested that the director's "preferred method of 'dealing with' the double is through a death fall in the presence of the hero"[16]—in artists' remakes of Hitchcock there is no such management of the double's presence precisely because the remake does not engage in an antagonistic stance towards the original. Unlike older paradigms of appropriation art, which aimed at subversion or critique of the cultural products they repurposed, the remakes produced beginning in the early 1990s can take on any number of positions towards the original, ranging from critique to homage, passing through blank repetition, and most often combining elements of all three. Works such as Dellsperger's *Body Double #4*, Douglas's *Subject to a Film: Marnie*, and Huyghe's *Remake,* all of which produce doubles of Hitchcock's films through reenactments of them, by no means critique or malign the director or his work. Rather, scenes and moments from Hitchcock's films appear reanimated, repeated with a difference that relies on the viewer's familiarity with the original and yet exploits it to eerie effect. These doublings are necessarily unfaithful, drawing out differences between the original and the remake. Rather than asserting sameness, *Schizo (Redux)*, as its title would suggest, draws out inconsistencies and contradictions between Van Sant's remake and Hitchcock's original. The emphasis is on the remake as a locus of transformation that aims not at fidelity but at the production of difference from within repetition.

In the artistic remakes of Hitchcock's films, as in the films themselves, the double is never a twin: it always occupies a different status or a different realm. The remake-as-double is inescapably belated, parasitic, and condemned to inferiority. Instead of defiantly rejecting this position only to fall deeper into it by trying to compete with the original (as so many Hollywood remakes have done), the remakes of contemporary art embrace these qualities and make them integral parts of the work. Huyghe's *Remake*, for example, was shot on poor-quality video in a barely furnished apartment, with amateur actors struggling to remember their lines. Instead of ordering dinner brought in from a fancy restaurant, Jeff and Lisa have soda and pizza. Huyghe replaces the Greenwich Village courtyard of the original with a construction site, as if to emphasize that *Remake* is about the labor of reenactment rather than any attempt at a polished, finished product that would somehow compete with or seek to replace *Rear Window*. *Remake* is much less about duplicating *Rear Window* than it is about examining how pre-existing cultural forms can provide inhabitable frameworks that will be recognizable as a shared memory.

Like the double, the fetish exists as an important component of Hitchcock's cinema that finds itself allegorized as the filmmaker is adapted to a gallery context. In Hitchcock's films, one finds everyday objects framed in close-up so as to be extracted from their surroundings and take on a strange allure. Fetishes in an anthropological rather than psychoanalytic sense, they are endowed with an almost supernatural power due to a specifically cinematic transformation of isolation and magnification. Whether it is the glowing white liquid of the glass of milk in *Suspicion* (1941) or the key of *Notorious*, many objects in Hitchcock's cinema protrude and fascinate beyond their narrative function. As Jean-Luc Godard expressed in the section of his *Histoire(s) du cinéma* (1989-98) devoted to Hitchcock, we may forget any number of plot details, but we will certainly remember "a row of bottles, a pair of glasses, a piece of music, a keychain." In art derived from Hitchcock, one finds a similar desire to parcel out the director's films into such possessable fragments and quasi-magical objects, as if to redouble Hitchcock's own treatment of privileged motifs in a more extreme fashion.

With the exception of Draeger's *Schizo (Redux)*, which can be watched start to finish with the story intact, the narratives of the host films are summarily eliminated in artist's remakes of Hitchcock. Instead, as if abiding by Godard's counsel, small components are isolated for close scrutiny. Artists isolate a part-object and have it stand in for the absent whole of the original film. Pfeiffer's *Self-Portrait as a Fountain*, Bernard's *Ask the Dusk* series, Gordon's *Empire*, and his *Souvenir of Non-Existence* all isolate and fixate on a particular part or element of a Hitchcock film. The slow crawl of *24 Hour Psycho* breaks the flow of the film to a series of near-still images, allowing the gallery visitor to grasp hold of each normally fleeting instant.[17] In *The Phoenix Tapes*, Girardet and Müller dismember Hitchcock's cinema and reconstitute a Frankensteinian film-body. In the video's second section, "Burden of Proof," the centrality of alluring objects in close-up is particularly highlighted through an encyclopaedic cataloguing of such shots. The chapter begins with a series of close-ups of objects bearing names or initials from *Frenzy, North by Northwest, Rebecca* (1940) *Strangers on a Train* (1951), and *Torn Curtain* (1966) before using Johnny Jones's monographed trunk from *Foreign Correspondent* (1940) to segue into a sequence about suitcases and packing. In turn, the suitcases metonymically link to a set of shots of briefcases, and so on. In these paradigmatic repetitions, Girardet and Müller bring together the many fetish objects of Hitchcock's cinema in order to emphasize their status as key sites of spectatorial investment. The action of remaking mimics and exaggerates a pre-existing quality of the films in question. The artists highlight how the iconographic richness of Hitchcock's recurring motifs trumps narrative progression, a feature of the director's *oeuvre* that certainly eases the transition of his work into the realm of visual art.

This desire to isolate a moment or object from a Hitchcock film might be see as a brutal urge to destroy the plenitude of the original. Indeed, Dominique Païni has described the recycling of old films as a kind of violence brought against the cinema, while the found-footage genre has been at certain junctures distinctly linked to a critique of mass-media representations.[18] However, the impulse to isolate privileged moments of a film is in fact endemic to cinephilia itself, insofar as Paul Willemen describes it as a mode of spectatorship that fixates on a single "epiphanic moment." "The cinephiliac discourse," in Willemen's words, "tends to work on scenes, on moments of gesture, on looks," rather than on the film as a whole.[19] Given that, as Thomas Leitch has persuasively argued, Hitchcock's films are perhaps best understood as collections of moments, they are especially suited to this form of cinephilic spectatorship and to its translation into artistic practice.[20] It would be misguided, then, to view the dissection of Hitchcock's films as an act necessarily endowed with a negative intent; cinephilic homage is just as likely, but ambivalence is perhaps most common. Whatever the stance taken, these artists construct relationships to Hitchcock's cinema that very much allegorize certain of its textual preoccupations. For these artists, Hitchcock inspires neither lionizing homage nor outright condemnation, but rather is representative of something else: an opportunity.

*   *   *   *   *

Hitchcock's films present artists with an unparalleled opportunity to reflect on the history and cultural place of a certain kind of cinema at a moment when a very different kind of cinema has taken its place. To venture another possible explanation as to why Hitchcock has been so popular in contemporary art, it is necessary to consider the director's particular place in film history and its relation to the state of cinema at the beginning of the twenty-first century. Fetishism is at play not only in the way in which Hitchcock's film are carved up for recontextualization; Hitchcock himself becomes an overvalued fetish object that is seized upon as the "just before" the loss of unchallenged cinematic hegemony, marking the moment that cinema began its competition with television. As a great auteur of classical Hollywood, he embodies an age of cinema now over and gone, looked back upon with some nostalgia as a reservoir of public experience and collective memory.

As noted above, narrative cinema was something of a "bad object" for artists until the beginning of the 1990s, a time that not coincidentally is marked by escalating fears concerning the fate of cinema in a new media ecology. Hitchcock famously suggested that "One of television's greatest contributions was that it brought murder back into the home where it belongs."[21] But television also initiated a privatization of cinema that has greatly intensified since and in relation to which one must consider the increased presence of cinema within the public space of the museum. It is no coincidence that the artistic fetishization of Hitchcock reaches full force in the mid-1990s, contemporaneous with the centennial of cinema, the digitization of moving images, and the popularization of the Internet. Much Hitchcock-related art makes use of the new possibilities of the digital image, but is simultaneously symptomatic of the melancholic notion that such novelties might "kill" the cinema. The illusionistic, narrative cinema of classical Hollywood is no longer a monolith to be refused, but rather an entity fit for commemoration. And yet on a very basic level, most of the works that make reference to Hitchcock rely on digital video: it is digital video that makes artists who sometimes have little formal training in filmmaking able to produce reenactments of Hitchcock's films and that allows them to sample and repurpose footage from Hitchcock's films. This creates new opportunities for artists and amateurs alike: one might say that that many artists' remakes of Hitchcock are professionalized commentaries on the new kinds of fan activity made possible by these technological changes. A quick YouTube search, for example, yields dozens of results of fan renditions of *Psycho*'s shower scene. In short, the tendency to remake Hitchcock's films beginning in the 1990s must be seen as both a part of and a response to the media convergence after digitization.

This reflection on the new mutability of cinema is one of the key attributes of contemporary artists' fascination with remaking cinema. Works such as Gordon's *24 Hour Psycho*, Campbell's *Illuminated Average #1: Hitchcock's Psycho*, and

Canogar's *Dial "M" For Murder* are as much about the technological changes that have recently affected cinema as they are about the films they appropriate. Campbell interrogates the transition to a digital cinema of calculation, while Gordon and Canogar work with the already outmoded medium of VHS tape. To confront these issues, these artists could choose any film. So why Hitchcock? Why pick these films to rework in this manner? The transformations cinema is undergoing in the digital era offer new aesthetic possibilities but also inspire a meditation on what might be lost. Hitchcock is an attractive emblem of this coexistence of excitement for the future and nostalgia for the past: the director is embraced as the embodiment of classical Hollywood, but, in his eager embrace of television, he simultaneously points to its loss of cultural dominance. Perhaps more than any other director, Hitchcock invokes questions of a competitive media environment and of cinema in transition due to new technologies and new media. His work in the 1950s and early 1960s constitutes a complex response to the disintegration of classical cinema in the face of television: he made a break with classicism and produced TV shows, but also participated in technological novelties designed to maintain the dominance of cinema, working not just with 3-D in *Dial M for Murder* (1954), but also the widescreen process of VistaVision in *To Catch A Thief* (1955), *Vertigo*, and *North by Northwest*. In other words, he played both sides of the struggle between cinema and television.

In Martijn Henriks's erasure of the birds of *The Birds* or in Daniel Pítin's paintings of that film, there is the sense that the artists are attracted to the way in which its special effects anticipate the painterly compositing that produces the fabricated images of today's digital cinema. *Avant la lettre,* Hitchcock was embracing a conception of the image that has today become dominant. When artists turn to films such as *Psycho*, *Dial M For Murder,* and *The Birds*—films in which the technological changes facing cinema in the mid-twentieth century were particularly visible—they telescope this earlier moment of change with their own. In remaking these films in particular, these artists bring together the challenge of television with the challenge of new media. Hitchcock is poised on the cusp between the cinema that existed before television and the cinema that would exist after it, straddling a moment of intense transition—precisely the sort of condition in which cinema finds itself once again at the turn of the twenty-first century, when a tremendous anxiety circulates around the fate of the institution. He is embraced for his dual status of being both an emblem of classical Hollywood and its demise.

The "Hitchcock of contemporary art" is in large part a reaction formation produced out of anxieties concerning the place of cinema in a digital age, monumentalizing the director as a stand-in for an entire repertoire of image production that has ceded its ground as film industries, technologies, and audiences have changed. But this anxiety around the fate of cinema is not new: it was present even during Hitchcock's *Cahiers* canonization. As Dudley Andrew has noted, French cinephilia at this time rebelled against *le cinéma de papa*, but it was also "a quiet, defensive war against another, less evident enemy: the disorganized, unaccredited, and unencumbered images beginning to pour out of television screens, in France and elsewhere."[22] The very concept of the auteur that took shape at *Cahiers*—one that Antoine de Baecque sees as precipitating the invention of "Hitchcock" as its greatest exemplar—arose in conjunction with and in reaction to the "unencumbered images" of TV, just as today's cinema of the museum finds formation in relation to a new anxiety about the relationship between cinema and digital media.[23] The fetishization of Hitchcock in contemporary art may be seen as the outgrowth of this earlier "war," one that was once perhaps "quiet" but that has become increasingly noisy in recent years as scores of articles in the popular and academic presses speculate melancholically on the future of cinema. Anthony McCall notes that "With Douglas Gordon's work, there is a strong element of nostalgia for a particular period of Hollywood, a classical period that never actually existed in fact."[24] This period of classical cinema may never have existed in the past, but it certainly exists in our present as a myth fabricated out of fears of the institution's future. Classical Hollywood cinema has shed the label of "bad object" it possessed for the artists of an earlier generation to become instead a lost object. And the figure that encapsulates these desires and anxieties perhaps more than any other is the Hitchcock of contemporary art.

*   *   *   *   *

If contemporary art is to look back nostalgically at a certain age of cinema, how will it discern which works in particular deserve commemoration? The revised film historical canon that appears in contemporary curatorial and artistic practice is very much a modernist one, running from Hitchcock to Antonioni to Brakhage. In *Hall of Mirrors: Art and Film Since 1945*, the film clips selected for inclusion could be grouped into four categories: movies about art, movies about movies and/or other media, modernist masterpieces from Europe and America, and experimental cinema. It is almost as if reflexivity—whether it regards the medium of film or the institution of cinema—is *the* attribute that renders even the most popular films as legible as "art" within the museum complex. Film may be forgiven for belonging to so-called "low culture," as long as it exhibits some self-consciousness about its cultural position and its representational strategies.

Such reflexivity is an attribute, of course, that is prominent in Hitchcock's cinema. Hitchcock ceaselessly delved into the very foundations of the classical system, questioning, among other things, its representations of female beauty and voyeuristic "regime of the keyhole."[25] He reflexively examined the very basis of our fascination with cinema while continuing to work in a popular idiom, at once complicit with and critical of the power structures and gender norms on display. Almost every Hitchcock film is to some degree a film about cinema itself. Yet unlike many experimental filmmakers, whose interrogations into the medium tended to focus on its material basis, Hitchcock interrogated the cinema as an ideological and social institution. This is of particular significance for artists today, as questions of how both media and perception function socially, historically, and libidinally have superseded the uniquely materialist investigations of medium specificity that marked the 1960s and 1970s. In order to engage with questions of vision and power, then, it is not surprising that contemporary artists do not turn to the reflexive materialism of a film like Peter Kubelka's *Arnulf Rainer* (1960) or Michael Snow's *Wavelength* (1967), but instead to Hitchcock.

Though Hitchcock was certainly not what French Impressionist film theorists had in mind when they advocated for a pure cinema that would no longer depend slavishly on literature, his narratives of vision and desire perpetually double back to address the very basis of the spectator's engagement with cinema. It is a practice that led Slavoj Žižek to remark that "One is even tempted to say that Hitchcock's films ultimately contain only two subject positions, that of the director and that of the viewer—all diegetic persons assume, by turns, one of these two positions."[26] If artists in the 1990s and 2000s become concerned with examining the structures of identification and economies of desire that are found in narrative cinema, Hitchcock's sustained interrogation of these issues make him the ideal conduit through which to do so.

Crucially, Hitchcock, more than many other filmmakers, blends this reflexivity with broad appeal, accessibility, and a recognizable imprimatur. The populism of his work is as or perhaps more important than his modernist impulses in explaining his prominent position in contemporary art. The return to classical Hollywood in the art since 1990 is very much engaged in reactivating an experience of collectivity stemming from a shared reception of media at a time when images are most often consumed individually and directed towards increasingly specific niche markets. As Whitney Museum curator Chrissie Iles has suggested, "Artists' use of film in the 1990s, particularly popular Hollywood film, is partly to do with wanting to engage with, and perhaps influence, the connective tissue that film creates, and participate in a common language of communication."[27]

Cynically, one could say this is a way of art appealing to a lowest common denominator and increasingly submitting to mass media norms; after all, it is certain that the mobilization of cinema in contemporary art is in some respects closely linked to an institutional desire for accessibility, spectacle, and entertainment value. Less cynically, one could say that this is a part of the insistence on participation and collectivity in the art of the 1990s, a tendency that arose in direct relation to the development of the Internet, which both compromised existing forms of social organization (largely face-to-face) and made possible new ones, such as the weak-tie networks of Twitter and Facebook. Both of these explanations ring true. In any case, this emphasis on cinema as a repository of shared cultural memory further accounts for why Hitchcock—and not Godard, Antonioni, or Straub/Huillet—is privileged over any other director in the art of this time. He accomplishes the perfect balancing act between modernist reflexivity and classical populism that suits the needs of contemporary art. In some cases, there is a sense that the artist knows very little about film history and cares about it even less; he or she is moving *through* it to activate another set of questions concerning publicity, collectivity, and belonging. The popular and iconic dimensions of Hitchcock's films are in this respect central, since the "connective tissue" they can generate amongst an anonymous public might not be as resilient if the references were to films more esoteric, less familiar.

*   *   *   *   *

This consideration of how one might characterize the Hitchcock of contemporary art will now turn to a recent video collage that in many ways functions as a meta-commentary on the entire tendency. Johan Grimonprez's *Double Take* is an eighty-minute video that weaves together tales of mistaken identity, of strange objects coming from the sky, and of the cinema—all themes dear to Hitchcock. In a

Figure 7. One of Hitchcock's doubles: celebrity
impersonator Ron Burrage. Johan Grimonprez, still
from *Looking for Alfred* (2004). Courtesy of the artist.

tremendous feat of analogical thinking, Grimonprez draws a
proliferation of doubles into a maelstrom of substitutions and
twinned likenesses that all find their common grounding in
the master of suspense (fig. 7). The artist places the director at
the nucleus of a de- and reconstructed history that examines
fear, catastrophe, and an anxiety over identity through clips
from movies, TV shows, televised news, and commercials.
Whereas most Hitchcock-related art confines itself to the
director's films, *Double Take* places him at the center of a much
larger inquiry that delves into Cold War paranoia, Borgesian
fiction, the introduction of television into the American home,
and the devastating events of September 11, 2001. Hitchcock is
a MacGuffin who sets in motion an investigation into how the
Cold War era initiated an industry of spectacularized fear that
persists today. Taking the existence of an artistic obsession
with Hitchcock as a given, *Double Take* works outward into a
broader socio-political context to probe what the stakes of such
an engagement with Hitchcock's films might be. Throughout
this work, many of the characteristics attributed in this essay to
the Hitchcock of contemporary art emerge: Grimonprez

cultivates references to Magritte and takes an interest in how Hitchcock's films have circulated throughout culture; Hitchcock's cinema finds many doubles and is carved up into fetishized moments; he emerges as a key player in cinema's war with television; and he is valued for his combination of reflexivity and accessibility, attractive precisely because of how many times he has been remade by himself and by others.

The work's opening sequence introduces the three lines of inquiry that dominate this often frenetic collage, each one a fable of the double. Grimonprez begins with a news report of the so-called "Kitchen Debate," a conversation between Richard Nixon and Nikita Khrushchev at the opening of the American National Exhibition in Moscow on July 24, 1959. Then, on the soundtrack, the recognizable voice of Hitchcock is heard. He is telling the anecdote of the MacGuffin, with Helen Scott translating his words into French so that Truffaut will be able to understand. This audio recording, culled from the interview sessions conducted in 1962, is paused, rewound, and played again as a celebrity voice impersonator endeavors to imitate the director's speech on a soundstage. Then countdown leader cuts to a clip of Hitchcock being photographed for a mug shot, taken from the introductory sequence of an *Alfred Hitchcock Presents* episode entitled "Number Twenty-Two" (1957). As Hitchcock is photographed wearing a pageboy cap, his "record" is read out: "1940, picked up on *Suspicion*. 1942, *Spellbound*. 1944, *Notorious*. 1955, *Rear Window*. 1956, *The Man Who Knew Too Much*." Notably (and perhaps unsurprisingly given the invariable ineptitude of the police in Hitchcock's films), the dates given here are all wrong, save for that of *The Man Who Knew Too Much*, which would have been in release at that time. As in many remakes of Hitchcock in contemporary art, the facts are replayed, but unfaithfully. The dialogue proceeds as follows:

DETECTIVE: Anything to say, Hitchcock?
HITCHCOCK *(affecting somewhat of a Cockney accent)*: Well sir, I maintained a good record but I'm trying to do better.

DETECTIVE: Better? Do you call this latest charge doing better—appearing on *television*?
HITCHCOCK: I'm sorry, sir, but my family was hungry.
DETECTIVE: Take him away!
HITCHCOCK: Wait a minute, sir! You've got the wrong man!

From this opening sequence, it is possible to identify three doublings of the mid-twentieth century that are braided together throughout *Double Take*: the Cold War relationship between the Soviet Union and the United States as articulated in the "Kitchen Debate," the performance of "Hitchcock" by the director and his impersonators, and the relationship between cinema and television.

After Hitchcock is dragged away by the policeman, a brief flash of televisual static hits the screen and gives way to the film's title card. A grainy shot of what appears to be Hitchcock's eye in close-up cuts to jerky handheld footage of an office interior rocked by an explosion. Then newsreel footage reports an army bomber crashing into the Empire State Building in 1945 and calls the event "a disaster that remains the most singular in New York City's history." A snowy long shot of a body hurtling through the air in slow motion is replayed twice before the sequence comes to a caesura on a milky white void, held for several seconds. A plane crashing into a Manhattan landmark in 1945 is said to be the most singular disaster in the city's history, but the shots that bookend the newsreel—the office interior and the falling bodies— invoke September 11, 2001, a day that surely wrested that title from the earlier plane-building collision. The falling bodies announce that though most of *Double Take* will hover in the mid-twentieth century, its interest in that period's intertwining of media, fear, and spectacle resides in the possibility of uncovering there the roots of our present condition. References to 9/11 bookend *Double Take*, suggesting the frame through which the spectator is invited to consider the video's mid-century montage.

This contemporary frame allows *Double Take* to look back on cinema as an old medium. It embraces cinema as a commonly shared set of images and narratives that may be used to explore a complex political field, but simultaneously suggests that it is an image regime of the past, superseded by newer media from the advent of television onward. As we continue to grapple with the implications of living in a networked world, *Double Take* returns us to the historical moment that Grimonprez sees as the end of the cinematic age and the beginning of the information age. This shift is conceived not simply as the passage from one dominant medium to another, but as nothing less than the passage from one episteme to the next. Crucially—and in a gesture that provides a great insight into what has been at stake in so many artists' remakes of classical cinema—Grimonprez insists that the logic of a particular medium provides a privileged way of comprehending the logic of the particular period in which that medium was dominant.

The primary narrative through-line of *Double Take* is a classic fable of the *doppelgänger*—a modernist motif dear to Hitchcock and perhaps most exemplified by the 1955 *Alfred Hitchcock Presents* episode that he directed, "The Case of Mr. Pelham." Grimonprez collaborated with novelist Tom McCarthy to produce a retelling of the Jorge Luis Borges short story, "The Other," in which a man meets an older double of himself. Interestingly, the Borges story is itself a remake: it not only exists in two versions (the alternate version entitled "25 August 1983"), but is also a retelling of Dostoyevsky's "The Double." Borges—born only eleven days after Hitchcock, in August 1899—weaves an impossible tale of self meeting self that McCarthy and Grimonprez transpose to the set of *The Birds* in 1962. Over a montage of clips of identical twins, a gruff English voice says, "They say that if you meet your double, you should kill him. Or that he will kill you. I can't remember, but the gist of it is that two of you is one too many." And so initiates a story straight out of Hitchcock: of murderous doubles, poisoned liquids, and clever retorts.

The story begins as Hitchcock is about to film his cameo appearance outside the pet shop when he is told he has a phone call waiting. He gives the cast and crew a twelve-minute break and proceeds to his office, on the way to which he has a strange encounter with the studio security guard, who swears that he had already gone inside. As Hitchcock (represented through an assemblage of found footage and new footage shot with Hitchcock look-alikes) walks down the corridor, the soundtrack from *Psycho* begins to play, evoking associations of spectrality and temporal dislocation. In his office a man is waiting for him, an aged alter ego who makes two disturbing claims: that he too is Hitchcock and that that the year is 1980, the year of Hitchcock's death. The two men test each other to make sure that they are both indeed the "real" Hitchcock, with the 1962 Hitch finally giving in to the eerie truth of the situation due to the remarkable knowledge possessed by the man from 1980.

The 1962 Hitchcock asks the 1980 Hitchcock who will win the Cold War, but the visitor from the future shrugs off the question as insignificant. Instead, he provides an explanation of how another war—that between cinema and television—will turn out: "Half the movie theatres in the country have closed down, television has killed cinema, broken it down into bite-sized chunks and swallowed it whole like birds devouring their own parent." This statement, with its description of cinema dismembered into bites—a homonym of the "bytes" of the information age—has striking resonances with the fate of cinema in the 1990s and 2000s even more than that of 1980. The invocation of cannibalism is especially apposite with regard to the many recyclings of Hitchcock during this period in both Internet fan culture and art. Many of the Hitchcock remakes in contemporary art may be read as symptomatic responses to uncertainties surrounding the fate of the institution of cinema in a digital age, but here symptom gives way to diagnosis and does so through a simile that makes use of the animal Hitchcock was engaging with most at the time: birds.

The year 1962 is important for *Double Take*, functioning as something of its temporal anchor. It is the year of the birth of Johan Grimonprez, the year of the Cuban Missile Crisis, the year Hitchcock shot *The Birds*, the year in which McCarthy's "double take" on "The Other" is set, and—so *Double Take* implies—the year that television trumped cinema. The medial prophecies told by the 1980 Hitchcock to his younger self form a central part of *Double Take*, which takes up the television-cinema fratricide as one of its key themes. Though the video includes references to Hitchcock's Cold War films *Topaz* (1969) and *Torn Curtain*, Grimonprez concentrates primarily on *Psycho, The Birds,* and the introductions the director provided for *Alfred Hitchcock Presents* and the *Alfred Hitchcock Hour*. Or one might say, Grimonprez concentrates on two media, cinema and television.

The portrait of cinema found in *Double Take* is one of a cinema under threat from its evil double, television. *The Birds* is understood to be an allegory of television's invasion into the home: as Grimonprez remarked in an interview, "*The Birds* has generated every possible contradictory interpretation by Hitchcock scholars . . . But, like the MacGuffin, they refuse interpretation. I went for *The Birds* to allude to Hitchcock's ambivalent relationship with television, and by way of a detour, to lead back to the theme of the double—in particular, television as cinema's 'double.' "[28] As the birds sweep across Bodega Bay to terrorize its citizens, somewhat curiously, no one turns on the television to get news of what might be happening. Angelo Restivo has rightfully asked, "Did audiences in 1963 wonder at all why the characters in the film fail to connect to the broadcast network?"[29] Television provides no help in combating the birds because television *is* the birds—or rather, it is one of the many meanings that may be attached to them. Television overtakes cinema "like birds devouring their own parent." Though *Psycho* might represent Hitchcock's decisive break with classical cinema—a possible reason it has attracted so many artists—for Grimonprez, *The Birds* is the crucial turning point because it explicitly thematizes television's invasion into the American home.

Through many excerpts from *Alfred Hitchcock Presents* and the *Alfred Hitchcock Hour, Double Take* investigates at length what Grimonprez termed "Hitchcock's ambivalent relationship with television." The video includes numerous clips of Hitchcock introducing commercials on his television shows, each time making jokes about the banality of the medium and its insufferable advertisements (e.g., "Television is like the American toaster—you push the button and the same thing pops up every time"), while also embracing it as an important extension of the Hitchcock brand. As the Hitchcock of 1980 says to the Hitchcock of 1962, "We helped hasten the format's rise to power." Though in an age of HBO, well-known actors and directors are no longer considered to be slumming it by working in television, in the early 1960s the situation was much different. Hitchcock's embrace of the TV at this time is unparalleled by other directors of his stature, and yet he never missed an opportunity to mock the medium. The crassness of television and its production of programs that will function as padding for the real moneymakers—the commercials—here ascend over the cinema, with Hitchcock ambivalently straddling the two.

Television invades the home, but what does it bring with it? As noted above, Hitchcock said that it brought murder, and Grimonprez does not disagree. *Double Take* finds a second allegorical meaning for *The Birds*, seeing in the film a fictional visualization of real anxieties around a threat from the sky. The video includes found footage of numerous new broadcasts speculating on the possibility of nuclear attack and the exploration of outer space. The opening sequence sets up 9/11 as the most recent incarnation of this persistent motif, but other examples recur throughout: hundreds of birds crash into the Empire State Building in 1948 and science fiction cycles about space invaders are offered as doubles of *The Birds*, functioning like so many fatal coincidences that all bring us circling back to Hitchcock.[30]

Throughout *Double Take*, the artist develops themes explored in his 1997 video, *Dial H-I-S-T-O-R-Y*, which dealt with the history of airplane hijackings in order to examine how the mass media function as a fear industry that spectacularizes catastrophe and perversely constitutes it as entertainment. Grimonprez is keenly interested in the Cold

War as the first war to take place more on the airwaves than on the battlefield. The "Kitchen Debate" is identified as the first televised summit, while the first televised presidential debate (between Kennedy and Nixon) and its famous medium-specific results also make an appearance.[31] In a rather Baudrillardian manner, the Cold War is proposed as the point at which reality becomes stranger than fiction and the two begin to intertwine to the point of indiscernibility. Even Hitchcock's cameo in *The Birds* is proposed as moment of such confusion, as a real person enters a fictional diegesis. Grimonprez links together an investigation of the rise of television with both the space race and the fear of nuclear war so as to point to the imbrication of politics and the media. *Double Take* employs a documentary-fiction hybrid to help explore how catastrophe is consumed as media entertainment and how documentary and fictional images become interchangeable with one another—a strategy evident in the decision to place opening shots from Hitchcock's *Topaz* into a montage of Cold War news footage. Though only three of Hitchcock's films reference the Cold War outright—*North by Northwest*, *Torn Curtain*, and *Topaz*—Grimonprez suggests that the whole of his *oeuvre* is produced for a society living in fear of nuclear war and communism alike. Through a tour of key flashpoints—such as Fidel Castro's visit to the Soviet Union and the Bay of Pigs invasion—as they were seen on television, Grimonprez explores how the media heated up the Cold War. In this way, our historical present appears as not so radically different from these mid-century debacles, for it was there that war first began to take on the guise of entertainment.

But remember: "If you meet your double, you should kill him." In the Dostoyevsky/Borges-inspired narrative, the Hitchcock of 1962 does indeed kill his *doppelgänger* by poisoning his cup of coffee, only to then grow old and become the Hitchcock of 1980 he had killed. But when the two are in conversation, one says to the other, "Who says there are only two of us? Maybe there are three or four of us." Rather than any pair of doubles, this proliferation of clones comes much closer to providing an accurate snapshot of the situation; there are

The reason for my lack of enthusiasm for this Alfred Hitchcock lookalike contest will be apparent when I tell you that I entered and was eliminated in the first round.

Figure 8. Still from *The Alfred Hitchcock Hour* as
featured in Johan Grimonprez, *Double Take* (2009).
Courtesy of Universal and the artist.

indeed many, many "Hitchcocks" today. *Double Take*
assiduously demonstrates their multiplication, whether it is
in the interviews with Ron Burrage, a professional Hitchcock
impersonator, or with the many excerpts of the introductions
to his television programs in which the director toys with his
identity. In one introduction, Hitchcock appears as the
puppet master, pulling the strings of a marionette Alfred
below him, while in another he holds a look-alike contest,
only to complain that he was eliminated in the first round
(fig. 8). Through these introductions and through his many
cameo appearances, the filmmaker of the double turns
himself into a series of simulacra behind which no single
original can be located.

One sees this move away from stable reference in the *The
Birds* as well: as noted above, its pioneering trick shots
foreshadow the predominance of compositing in digital
cinema, while the semiotic instability of its title animals
suggests an increased mutability of meaning. *The Birds* moves
far beyond the modernist fable of the *doppelgänger* to represent
instead an anonymous, inhuman antagonist who strikes

without clear motivation. This post-classical Hitchcock is held up as an early representative of the cultural logic that began with television and which continues in an exacerbated fashion into the twenty-first century. Though the double may be the titular trope of *Double Take*, one double leads to another and another throughout, seemingly *ad infinitum,* in a mesmerizing hall of mirrors of that breaks away from the two into the many. The sheer allegorical promiscuity of the work enacts on a formal level the insufficiency of the double, that trope so closely aligned with both modernity and cinema. Instead the video constructs a network in which everything is like everything else, information piles up and piles up, and the real and the fictional become indistinguishable. This hypertrophy of meaning reverses into babbling meaninglessness, as identity disintegrates into serially exchangeable likenesses.

Through the final credits of *Double Take*, a rapid montage of the fall of the Berlin Wall, a clip of *Independence Day* (1996), successive heads of state from the United States and Russia shaking hands as if in reconciliation (Reagan/Gorbachev, Clinton/Yeltsin, Bush/Putin), and ends with former Secretary of Defence Donald Rumsfeld and his (in)famous statement of February 12, 2002, concerning the situation in Afghanistan after the U.S.-led invasion:

> Reports that say that something hasn't happened are always interesting to me, because as we know, there are known knowns; there are things we know we know. We also know there are known unknowns; that is to say we know there are some things we do not know. But there are also unknown unknowns—the ones we don't know we don't know.[32]

By ending *Double Take* with this very post-9/11 statement, Grimonprez returns the viewer to the image of falling bodies that had functioned as a caesura in the video's opening montage. Grimonprez has said that he believes an "ontological shift" occurred with 9/11, one that reconfigured the relationship between reality and fiction:

At that point, there were already so many images out
there in the world, in Hollywood, and in the media,
that mimicked the event. When we saw 9/11 live on
television, we looked at it as if it were unreal, as if
fiction were running ahead of reality.[33]

The entirety of *Double Take* is invested in excavating the
formative moments of this condition, finding in Hitchcock a
figure who presided over the transitions from what
Baudrillard would term the age of representation to the age
of simulation.[34] Either/or, us/them, and true/false are
distinctions that no longer apply. Instead, we inhabit a
dispersed and flexible network of circulating signs
unmoored from stable reference.

   Despite its status as a media event of enormous
proportions, September 11, 2001 was, of course, by no
means unreal. Perhaps the most problematic aspect of
Double Take is how close it comes to asserting that the real
has simply receded into media simulation.[35] There is little
attentiveness to the possible violence that lurks in the action
of asserting one thing as a parallel to or precursor of
another. For Grimonprez, the cloning of Hitchcock that has
taken place in the many critical, filmic, and artistic
remakings of the director's work serves as an analogy for a
shift from a locatable referent to a chain of simulacra linked
together in a global network: "I thought there was an
interesting analogy; Hitchcock has become monstrously big,
just like fear and catastrophe."[36] Hitchcock himself is "the
man who knew too much," presciently understanding this
cultural logic through his play with identity and his
vanguard meditation on the fears it elicits in *The Birds*. If
much of the manipulation of found footage, the amateur
reenactments, and the iconographic interrogations that have
dominated engagements with Hitchcock in contemporary
art staged a nostalgic return to an earlier cultural and
representational system, Grimonprez interrogates precisely
what might be at stake in this gesture. He unfolds the
precise nature of Hitchcock's status as a transitional figure

between this era and our own and, in so doing, claims that the director and his films serve as points at which the broader movements of history and the affective state of a population become visible.

*   *   *   *   *

In the work of Grimonprez and many other artists who have embraced Hitchcock, the differing representational and epistemological possibilities of old and new media are closely linked to an implicit periodization of an old and a new epoch. As one medium gives way to another, so too is one way of understanding the world displaced by another. Though cinema continues to mean many things to many people, the assumption in the artworks that make reference to Hitchcock is that we are living in a definitively post-cinematic era, one marked by changing media formations as much as by evolving forms of social organization and different conceptions of subjectivity. In many of these works one finds a distinct nostalgia for an earlier age of cinema and everything that went along with it. And yet the projected images of remembered movies that have filled museums and galleries over the past two decades are not simply a retreat into a lost past. The revivification of Hitchcock provides a means of telescoping an earlier moment of transition with our own, not only to memorialize the obsolete but also to interrogate the new possibilities made available by a new cinema, one that is not locked in a death-match with the digital, but one that is *already* digital. Contemporary artists approach Hitchcock's cinema as a lost image-regime in a digital era and as a lost locus of public experience in an era of privatization and individualized consumption, but their very opportunity to do so is largely thanks to digital means. Just like Hitchcock before them, they are playing both sides of the media tug of war.

Instead of any one-to-one relationship between an original Hitchcock film and an artist's copy, there is an acknowledgement that Hitchcock's films and the artworks derived from them circulate within a vast network of signs and are constantly subject to rethinking and recontextualization. In this sense, Grimonprez's visualization of the relationship to Hitchcock as many-to-many rather than one-to-one constitutes another way in which *Double Take* reflects on the recent spate of Hitchcock remakes. While his invocation of the simulacrum in relation to September 11, 2001 exhibits a careless indulgence in a certain variety of theoretical discourse, as a description of how one understands the circulation of the Hitchcock brand today, it is strikingly accurate. Across the many appropriations of the director in contemporary art there is an implicit acknowledgement that there is no one "Hitchcock" to which one might return—no biographical person and no single interpretation of his films— and he is all the more attractive for it.

The same goes for the cinema itself, of which Hitchcock is so frequently a synecdochic marker: the pure object of an omnipotent cinema unthreatened by television is long gone, if it ever existed at all. On the contrary, it is in fact out of the cinema's dethroned and fragmented state that creative opportunities arise. Despite the melancholic gaze these remakes sometimes cast on the era of classical Hollywood, the Hitchcock of contemporary art is very much a contaminated, intermedial Hitchcock. If a work like *24 Hour Psycho* monumentalizes its source film, it does so as it undergoes rigor mortis and is subject to the double translation of VHS and the museum space. If cinema still occupied the hegemonic cultural position that it did throughout the bulk of Hitchcock's career, it would surely remain banished from the rarefied spaces of art, or at the very least admitted only to come under harsh critique. It is the disintegration and relative weakness of cinema today that brings artists back to Hitchcock and makes cinema fit for the gallery. In Hitchcock, artists find a director who fully actualized and interrogated the cinema's powers at a time when the medium was at its height of popularity and influence. He stands in as the last representative of Hollywood classicism, fastened onto in order to excavate the cultural place of cinema (both then and now) while grieving its loss.

But as much as Hitchcock is held up as exemplary of the classical Hollywood cinema, artists' interest in him equally depends on his departures from it—the ways in which he bears witness to its dissolution, the ways in which he broke its rules, and the ways in which he introduced a modernist reflexivity and personal stamp at the heart of an industrial and commercial form of cinema. Artists see in Hitchcock a director who anticipated that changes were afoot. The so-called "death of cinema" never really means the death of all cinema, but the death of a certain, historically-grounded idea of cinema. Hitchcock saw several of these ideas of cinema come and go in his career, and now, albeit posthumously, he is overseeing another: the birth of a vibrant cinema of the gallery and museum, which both memorializes the history of what cinema has been in the past and contributes to what it will be in years to come.

Notes

An earlier version of this paper was presented at the 2010 Society for Cinema and Media Studies Conference in Los Angeles. Many thanks to the participants and the attendees of the panel "Performing Under Duress: Voice, Expression, and Cultural Struggle in Hitchcock's Films," chaired by Susan White. Given the restricted circulation of these artworks, special thanks to Catherine Clark Gallery, David Zwirner Gallery, Christoph Draeger, Christoph Girardet, Johan Grimonprez, Marian Goodman Gallery, Matthias Müller, Sean Kelly Gallery, Thomas Erben Gallery, and Zapomatik for making them available to me.

1. Throughout the twentieth century, found-footage filmmakers made use of educational and scientific films, stock footage, advertisements, and footage of which the filmmaker may not have known the provenance much more frequently than identifiable images. This is closely tied to the material restrictions of working on film rather than video. It is in the 1990s that the ability to obtain cheap video and DVD copies of popular films allowed artists to recycle them without running up against the barriers of cost or accessibility that would previously have been faced.

2. For catalogs related to these exhibitions, see *Art and Film Since 1945: Hall of Mirrors*, ed. Kerry Brougher and Russell Ferguson, (Los Angeles: Museum of Contemporary Art, 1996); *Hitchcock et l'art: coïncidences fatales*, ed. Guy Cogeval and Dominique Païni (Milan: Edizioni Gabriele Mazzotta, 2000); *Notorious: Hitchcock and Contemporary Art*, ed. Kerry Brougher and Michael Tarantino, (Oxford: Museum of Modern Art, 1999); *Obsessionen: Die Alptraumfabrik des Alfred Hitchcock*, ed. Sabine Lenk (Marburg: Schüren, 2000); *Spellbound: Art and Film*, ed. Ian Christie and Philip Dodd (London: BFI Publishing, 2006).

3. For a list of "Hitchcocks," see Thomas Elsaesser, "Casting Around: Hitchcock's Absence," in *Johan Grimonprez: Looking for Alfred*, ed. Steven Bode (London: Hatje Cantz and Film and Video Umbrella, 2007), 140.

4. Richard Allen, "Introduction" to "Gus Van Sant vs. Alfred Hitchcock: A *Psycho* Dossier," *Hitchcock Annual*, 10 (2001-02), 125.

5. Christy Lange notes that though the work was originally produced using this VCR, in recent years, the work has been digitized and its slow motion regulated by a computer. See "Douglas Gordon: Ten Years Ago Today," *theanyspacewhatever*, ed. Nancy Spector (New York: Solomon R. Guggenheim Museum, 2008), 70.

6. It appears that Gordon took steps to ensure that the letter was returned to him rather than delivered to a random New York City resident. If had been delivered, how would it then be sold as art? One iteration of the project provides the address "2nd Left Rear, 125 West 9th Street, Chelsea, New York, USA," without a zip code. Another, with the return dated 27 May 1993, leaves out the street address entirely (though it is included on the letter inside), specifying only "2nd Left Rear, Chelsea, New York, USA." In both cases, the addresses are incomplete, thus resulting in Gordon's desired result of "return to sender."

7. See Hans-Ulrich Obrist, *Interviews, Volume 1* (Milan: Charta, 2003), 322.

8. The other films are *Breathless* (*À bout de souffle*, 1960), *Dirty Harry* (1971), *Dr. No* (1962), *Goodfellas* (1990), *The Magnificent Seven* (1960), and *Highlander* (1986).

9. For a detailed discussion of *The Phoenix Tapes*, see Federico Windhausen, "Hitchcock and the Found-Footage Installation: Müller and Girardet's *The Phoenix Tapes*," *Hitchcock Annual*, 12 (2003-04): 100-25, and Rembert Hüser, "QWERTY Cinema: Girardet/Müller's *Phoenix Tapes*," in *After the Avant-Garde: Contemporary German and*

Austrian Experimental Film, ed. Randall Halle and Reinhild Steingröver (Rochester, NY: Camden House, 2008): 245-68.

10. See Braxton Soderman, "The Index and the Algorithm," *differences: a journal of feminist and cultural studies*, 18, no. 1 (2007): 153-55.

11. Mark Peranson, "If You Meet Your Double, You Should Kill Him: Johan Grimonprez on *Double Take*," *Cinemascope*, no. 38 (April 2009); available online at www.cinemascope.com/cs38/int_peranson_grimonprez.html.

12. Stan Douglas was born in 1960, Douglas Gordon in 1966, Johan Grimonprez in 1962, Christoph Girardet in 1966, Pierre Huyghe in 1962, and Matthias Müller in 1961.

13. Dominique Païni, *Le temps exposé: Le cinéma de la salle au musée* (Paris: Cahiers du cinéma, 2002), 15; translation mine, emphasis in original.

14. On Hitchcock's enduring influence, see *After Hitchcock: Imitation, Influence, and Intertextuality*, ed. David Boyd and R. Barton Palmer (Austin: University of Texas Press, 2006), and Richard Allen "Hitchcock's Legacy," *A Companion to Hitchcock Studies*, ed. Leland Poague and Thomas Leach (Chichester: Wiley-Blackwell, 2011), 572-91.

15. On the use of painting in Hitchcock's films, see Stephen Heath, "Narrative Space," in *Narrative, Apparatus, Ideology: A Film Theory Reader,* ed. Philip Rosen (New York: Columbia University Press, 1986), 379-83, and Brigitte Peucker, *The Material Image: Art and the Real in Film* (Palo Alto: Stanford University Press, 2007), 68-103.

16. Michael Walker, *Hitchcock's Motifs* (Amsterdam: University of Amsterdam Press, 2005), 49.

17. This desire was in fact central to the genesis of the work. Douglas Gordon has stated, "In 1992 I had come home to see my family for Christmas and I was looking at a video of the TV transmission of *Psycho*. And in the part where Norman (Anthony Perkins) lifts up the painting of *Susanna and the Elders* and you see the close-up of his eye looking through the peep-hole at Marion (Janet Leigh) undressing, I thought I saw her unhooking her bra. I didn't remember seeing that in the VCR version and thought it was strange, in terms of censorship, that more would be shown on TV than in the video so I looked at that bit with the freeze-frame button, to see if it was really there." See Douglas Gordon, quoted in Amy Taubin, "*24 Hour Psycho*," *Spellbound: Art and Film*, ed. Ian Christie and Philip Dodd (London: BFI Publishing, 2006), 70.

18. See Dominique Païni, *Le temps exposé: le cinéma de la salle au musée* (Paris: Cahiers du cinéma, 2002), 67.

19. Paul Willemen, "Through the Glass Darkly: Cinephilia Reconsidered," in *Looks and Frictions: Essays in Cultural Studies and Film Theory* (Bloomington: Indiana University Press, 1994), 235.

20. Thomas M. Leitch, "The Hitchcock Moment," in *Framing Hitchcock: Selected Essays from the Hitchcock Annual*, ed. Sidney Gottlieb and Christopher Brookhouse (Detroit: Wayne State University Press, 2002), 180-96.

21. Alfred Hitchcock, "After-Dinner Speech at the Screen Producers Guild Dinner," in *Hitchcock on Hitchcock: Selected Writings and Interviews*, ed. Sidney Gottlieb (Berkeley: University of California Press, 1995), 58.

22. Dudley Andrew, "Jules, Jim, and Walter Benjamin," in *The Image in Dispute: Art and Cinema in the Age of Photography*, ed. Dudley Andrew (Austin: University of Texas Press, 1997), 35.

23. "It is certain that Hitchcock is the absolute master of this idea of cinema [the *Cahiers* auteur]. But this wasn't evident in 1955: Hitchcock was *invented* by these 'young turks.' " Antoine de Baecque, *La cinéphilie: Invention d'un regard, histoire d'une culture: 1944-1968* (Paris: Librairie Arthème Fayard, 2003), 26; translation mine, emphasis in original.

24. Anthony McCall, quoted in "Round Table: The Projected Image in Art," *October*, no. 104 (spring 2003), 86.

25. The term "regime of the keyhole" is borrowed from Christian Metz, *The Imaginary Signifier: Psychoanalysis and the Cinema*, trans. Celia Britton, Annwyl Williams, Ben Brewster, and Alfred Guzzetti (Bloomington: Indiana University Press, 1982), 95.

26. Slavoj Žižek, " 'In His Bold Gaze My Ruin is Writ Large,' " *Everything You've Always Wanted to Know about Jacques Lacan . . . But Were Afraid to Ask Hitchcock*, ed. Slavoj Žižek (London: Verso, 1992), 218.

27. Chrissie Iles, quoted in "Round Table: The Projected Image in Contemporary Art," 73.

28. Johan Grimonprez, quoted in Chris Darke, "Hitchcock is not himself today . . . : Johan Grimonprez in Conversation with Chris Darke," in *Johan Grimonprez: Looking for Alfred*, ed. Steven Bode (London: Hatje Cantz and Film and Video Umbrella, 2007), 81-83.

29. Angelo Restivo, "The Silence of *The Birds*: Sound Aesthetics of Public Space in Later Hitchcock," in *Hitchcock: Past and Future*, ed. Richard Allen and Sam Ishii-Gonzáles (London: Routledge, 2004), 176.

30. Slavoj Žižek has made the same comparison: "Is the endlessly repeated shot of the plane approaching and hitting the second WTC tower not the real-life version of the famous scene from Hitchcock's *Birds*, superbly analyzed by Raymond Bellour, in which Melanie approaches the Bodega Bay pier after crossing the bay on the small boat? When, while approaching the wharf, she waves to her (future) lover, a single bird (first perceived as an undistinguished dark blot) unexpectedly enters the frame from above right and hits her head. Was the plane which hit the WTC tower not literally the ultimate Hitchcockian blot, the anamorphic stain which denaturalized the idyllic well-known New York landscape?" See *Welcome to the Desert of the Real!: Five Essays on September 11 and Related Dates* (London: Verso, 2002), 14-15.

31. Radio listeners reportedly believed that Nixon had won the debate, while television viewers believed that Kennedy had won, suggesting the profound impact the new presence of television might have on American political outcomes.

32. Donald Rumsfeld, quoted in: "DoD News Briefing—Secretary Rumsfeld and General Myers" (12 February 2002), available online at www.defenselink.mil/transcripts/transcript. aspx?transcriptid=2636.

33. Johan Grimonprez, quoted in Niels van Tomme, "Constructing Histories: Johan Grimonprez Discusses *Double Take*," *Art Papers* (May/June 2009), 25-26.

34. See Jean Baudrillard, "Simulacra and Simulations," *Basic Writings*, ed. Mark Poster, second edition (Stanford: Stanford University Press, 2001), 173.

35. "To speak of reality becoming a spectacle is a breathtaking provincialism. It universalizes the viewing habits of a small, educated population living in the rich part of the world, where news has been converted into entertainment. . . . It suggests, perversely, unseriously, that there is no real suffering in the world." Susan Sontag, *Regarding the Pain of Others* (New York: Picador, 2003), 110.

36. Van Tomme, "Constructing Histories: Johan Grimonprez Discusses *Double Take*," 26.

GERGELY HUBAI

"Murder Can Be Fun": The Lost Music of Frenzy

"I had this composer in London; it was a film about a murder, and I wanted something whimsical. I gave him some instructions on the way the score should be. I went to the recording session, and the composer had every double bassoon and timpani in the city of London capable of making a lugubrious, ominous sound playing the music." "Mr. Hitchcock, for a film about a murder, this sounds very appropriate." "Well, Mr. Williams, you don't understand, murder can be fun."[1]

The exchange quoted above supposedly took place between Alfred Hitchcock and John Williams during their work on the director's last movie, *Family Plot*. Fresh off the success of his work on Steven Spielberg's *Jaws*, Williams was no novice in the game of film scoring, and he had his own distinct ideas about the musical needs of *Family Plot*. The director felt that it was very important to bring more light-heartedness to the music and the best advice he could give was to tell the composer what he explicitly wanted to avoid. The above anecdote could very well apply to Henry Mancini, who wrote the original music for *Frenzy* (1972).[2] Hitchcock was so dissatisfied that he ended up rejecting the work and eventually commissioned another score from British composer Ron Goodwin, the merits of which are discussed in Jack Sullivan's *Hitchcock's Music*.[3] Mancini's score, however, is a part of film music lore and deserves further examination.

Frenzy wasn't the first time Hitchcock rejected a score. His falling out with Bernard Herrmann during their work on *Torn*

Curtain was much more widely publicized and the music itself gained some cult following. It had two excellent re-recordings, conducted by Elmer Bernstein and Joel McNeely, and even though the music was never attached to the picture, the themes from the score had a life of their own. Herrmann himself reused some of the music in *The Battle of Neretva* (1971), and Elmer Bernstein utilized some of the rejected music in *Airplane!* (1980) and Martin Scorsese's *Cape Fear* (1991).[4] The score's influence can even be felt in such seminal works as Christopher Young's music for *Torment* (1986), where the use of bass flutes was a direct homage to the unused *Torn Curtain* score.[5] In contrast, little is known about Mancini's unused *Frenzy*. Even some of the most reliable sources do not confirm whether or not it was even recorded. The nature and the style of the music are occasionally discussed, yet critics are ready to compare Goodwin's and Mancini's versions without hearing the rejected score. Their judgments are based on knowledge about the *Pink Panther* composer's trademark song score style, but few can imagine how far off the mark their guesses are about what he did in his work on *Frenzy*.[6]

I aim to put the study of Henry Mancini's rejected *Frenzy* score on more solid footing, and organize my presentation in two sections. The first part describes the creation of this work and provides behind-the-scenes information from the composer himself, while the second part aims to give an overview of the unused music and how it differs from Ron Goodwin's work. For this latter part, I use the original manuscripts, which were kindly provided for my research by the Henry Mancini Estate. Using this material, I provide a full rundown of the fourteen cues Mancini recorded in the middle of December 1971. But first we must examine how this composer, best known for his amusing Blake Edwards scores, was hired for this very bleak thriller in the first place.

Historical Background

Mancini himself documented his work with Hitchcock, telling his story to Tony Thomas for his book *Film Music* and later reprinting the same material in his autobiography, *Did*

They Mention the Music?[7] The memories paint quite a different picture of Hitchcock than what we're used to from the director's own interviews or even Jack Sullivan's book, but Mancini's memories never contradict the material housed at the Margaret Herrick Library. In fact, the composer's reminiscences nicely complement familiar details about his association with *Frenzy*. An important question for the contemporary reader is why Hitchcock thought about hiring Mancini in the first place. We're of course talking about the composer who wrote the immortal "Pink Panther Theme" for Blake Edwards's series, "Moon River" for *Breakfast at Tiffany's* (1961) and the "Baby Elephant Walk" for *Hatari!* (1962). This is just a brief selection from Mancini's extensive filmography, which in fact included a substantial number of darker titles as well as these more well-known light pieces.

The composer began his career as a contract composer for Universal, providing individual cues for various horror pictures alongside such studio notables as Herman Stein and Irving Gertz. Mancini's first film composition was written for a scene in *Lost in Alaska* (1952), where he wrote a tumultuous piece for a sequence featuring Lou Costello getting pinched by a crab.[8] Mancini's further compositions could be found in dozens of other Universal creature features, including such cult fan favorites as *The Creature from the Black Lagoon* (1954), *It Came from Outer Space* (1953), and *Tarantula* (1955), and he crowned his days at the studio by writing music for Orson Welles's *Touch of Evil* (1958). Mancini's association with Blake Edwards brought him more frothy commissions, eventually pigeon-holing the composer as one who worked on comedies and wrote popular hit tunes. But despite being linked to a very specific genre, Mancini loved to work on all types of movies, so considering that *Frenzy* was being made at Universal, the composer's selection for the project doesn't seem to be such a strange choice after all.

According to his autobiography, Mancini had some discussions with Hitchcock about the score, but the records at Margaret Herrick Library give very little detail about the creative aspects of the collaboration. If there were distinct creative choices made about the tone and nature of each cue, very little of it survived in writing apart from the customary music measurement sheets, which detailed the intended positions of the cues. There's also surprisingly little information about the spotting, the process of selecting which scenes should go with and without music. Instead of this, the documents at the Herrick Library contain such financial tidbits as Mancini's flat fee for the commission (which was $25,000) and the fact that the composer himself was supposed to pay for his trip to London, including the cost of transportation to and from and accommodations in the British capital.[9] Mancini supposedly received his music measurement sheets by 23 November 1971, but the papers in his own collection reveal that he had already written some cues by this point. The music itself was recorded in the middle of December during four recording sessions, each of which lasted for three hours. Mancini remembered this occasion in the following way:

> We scored *Frenzy* in London, and Hitchcock was there throughout the recording session, which I found disconcerting. It was not so much a matter of his being there as that he didn't say much when we were doing it. He sat through every piece and nodded approval, and finally, when he was alone in the dubbing room, he decided that it didn't work. His reason for thinking so, I was told, was that the score was macabre, which puzzled me because it was a film with many macabre things in it. It wasn't an easy decision to accept, and it was crushing when it happened, but I thereupon joined a very exclusive club, the composers-with-scores-dumped club.[10]

This "club" of course wasn't that exclusive: according to a saying attributed to David Raksin, you weren't even a real film composer until you had one of your scores rejected. Nobody could elaborate on this more than Ron Goodwin, who himself replaced Sir William Walton when the United Artists brass fired the composer from *The Battle of Britain*

(1969).[11] The British composer worked a lot more closely with Hitchcock. Unlike Mancini, he received written instructions, which can be found in the Margaret Herrick Library. These notes were very specific about every audio aspect of the movie, and they suggest that Hitchcock looked at the Mancini score as a failed experiment: many of the instructions aim to do the exact opposite of what was done in the first score.[12] When a director is revered for his attention to detail as much as Hitchcock is, it's hard to imagine how he wound up with an entire score that in his opinion did so many things wrong. Scenes that had music now memorably play with silence, while sequences featuring Goodwin's cues weren't covered with music by Mancini. Could the disagreement be attributed to a lack of proper communication between the director and his composer? According to Henry Mancini, this was exactly the case:

> If I were doing the score again, I really don't know what I would do differently. It turned out that Hitchcock wanted a lighter score, which also confused me, because he and I discussed the musical requirements beforehand, and seemed to be in agreement. He afterwards hired Ron Goodwin, who is a friend of mine and with whom I later discussed the situation. Ron read me a detailed analysis of what Hitchcock had in mind after he decided he wanted another score. It was interesting, because I wish I had been given something like that to go by. It might have been a different story. But it was quite an experience.[13]

As mentioned earlier, nobody apart from Mancini and Hitchcock knew what the music sounded like. Only the director knew why he was so dissatisfied with the score, and unfortunately he never went on record to explain the exact reasons why he rejected it. Sullivan's discussion of the matter quickly cuts to the end of the story and quotes the last mention of Mancini from the *Frenzy* files: "No Mancini music was used. Ron Goodwin did the music, for which Mr. Hitchcock dictated new musical notes."[14] Even Bernard

Herrmann was ready to give his opinion: "Hitchcock came to the recording session, listened awhile and said 'Look, if I wanted Herrmann, I'd asked Herrmann. Where's Mancini?' He wanted a pop score from this Academy Award-winning song writer, and Mancini wrote what he thought was one."[15] These throwaway remarks eventually turned out to be the most often-quoted comments about the rejected music, but Herrmann's thoughts on the subject could reveal a more critical attitude on Herrmann's part, given our new knowledge about what the score sounded like.

At this time the composer was not on speaking terms with Hitchcock. The two never communicated after the *Torn Curtain* mishap. Still, Herrmann remained very passionate about Hitchcock and these strong feelings often colored his perception of other composers. In a 1970 interview, Herrmann depicted Maurice Jarre as an amateur whose music was ghostwritten for him. The French composer's response was that Herrmann may have been jealous of him for working with Hitchcock on *Topaz*.[16] It seems Mancini's rejection had the opposite effect and made Herrmann his comrade in rejection, but the above comments about the firing of Mancini that appeared in Donald Spoto's *The Dark Side of Genius* should still be taken with a grain of salt. Herrmann made his claims without any direct knowledge of the details of Mancini's score or his dealings with Hitchcock. But perhaps assuming that the score was not pop music, it may be that Herrmann recast his own dismissal from *Torn Curtain* and thought that the exact same thing happened with Mancini.[17] It is strange to note that while his break with Hitchcock left Herrmann with a bitter aftertaste, Mancini was left with some nice memories, especially of culinary delicacies:

> Apart from the film, I found Mr. Hitchcock to be a gracious and generous man. During lunch one day, we got into a discussion about a mutual interest we had, wine. The next day, a case of Chateau Haut Brion—magnums—was delivered to me. Come to thing of it, I guess the whole adventure was not a total

loss after all. I still think what I did on *Frenzy* was good—a score complete without themes, because it seemed to me the film didn't require any.[18]

To paraphrase the often-quoted description of the rejected score, Mancini's music is nothing like Herrmann's, but it is nothing like what we've come to expect from Mancini either. It is a bleak, uncompromising, and tuneless score with no real recurring themes apart from a few brief melodic ideas to tie it together. Gone too is Mancini's lush and popular song score style. Only two source cues contain hints of the composer's more leisurely sound which everybody knows. So what is the rest of the music really like?

The Lost Score

The following description and analysis of the music is based on the original sketches stored by the Henry Mancini Estate (this is not to be confused with UCLA's Henry Mancini's Collection, which houses material from between 1955 and 1969). The estate did not retain any recordings of the music itself, so I had to work from the composer's sketches, which were restored for me by Christian Téxier. Mancini's sketches usually had the music put down in 3-6 lines, with the exception of the "Main Title," which used a fuller orchestra and had a more detailed sketch utilizing 16 lines.[19] The sketches also contain exact timings for every cue apart from two pieces of source music, which are named thusly because they appear in the movie's diegesis (usually coming from some kind of on-screen source, such as a radio or a band playing on screen). These particular pieces were recorded wild; that is, they were not synchronized to the picture, like regular score cues. A separate document contains the intended orchestration, which I will draw from to convey the nature of the score itself.[20]

I have attempted to reconstruct the placement of the cues in the movie. This process was aided by three elements in the archival material. The cues were originally preserved in order of completion, which didn't necessarily correspond to the film order. This problem, however, was quickly resolved by the slate numbers. Slate numbers (such as 1M1) are used in every film score and indicate each cue's placement in the film. If the "Main Title" is labeled M-101, M means "music" and 101 means that the designated piece is the first cue in the picture's first reel. M-102 is the second piece in the first reel, and so on. M-302/400 means that the cue ran over a reel change. The second thing that made the reconstruction easier was Mancini's vivid cue titles, which are very helpful in placing the scenes as well as providing a giggle or two for those who know more about the composer's body of work. (I illustrate some of these inside jokes later in my essay.) The third element that helped in the reconstruction was Mancini's own synch-points, which were marked at the top of each sketch. While they were usually oblique, knowing the rough position of the cues was enough to find the definite timings for each and every piece, allowing for a comparison of how Mancini's score would have created much different effects from Goodwin's.[21]

In the following sections I include the title of each cue, specific information about its placement in the film, duration, and orchestration, and a brief commentary.

1. Main Title [M-101]

2:18/2:33, 55/61 measures. Orchestration: Organ 4 Clarinets, 4 Bassoons, 4 French Horns, 16 Violins, 10 Violas, 10 Celli, 6 Basses, Timpani [The two timings indicate a shorter and a longer version with an added opening fanfare.]

Most film score fans are already familiar with the "Main Title" piece, this being the only bit of Mancini's music for *Frenzy* commercially available. There was a re-recording done for the RCA collection called *Mancini in Surround* (1990), which contained other re-recorded excerpts from Mancini's old Universal pictures (*The Creature from the Black Lagoon, It Came from Outer Space, Tarantula*) and some of his later works, most of which are surprisingly still unavailable outside this collection (*Sunset, Mommie Dearest, The Prisoner of Zenda*). The "Main Title" of the rejected *Frenzy* score is certainly a revelation for fans of the movie, but it is also quite misleading, since the main title has almost nothing to do with the rest of the score. It is a magnificent piece in its own right, but the common speculation that this Gothic mood characterized the tone of the entire underscore is far from the truth. In its own way, this is a brilliant composition as a dark overture for a bleak movie, but it went against Hitchcock's intentions (which admittedly, were only articulated after the failed recordings with Mancini).

In his notes to composer Ron Goodwin, Hitchcock emphasized the fact that he wanted to juxtapose the opening music with the upcoming horrible murder, hence he requested an almost comically patriotic piece underscoring the panoramic opening shots of London. Goodwin, who cut his teeth with grandiose marches in movies like *Operation Crossbow* (1965) and *Where Eagles Dare* (1968), provided a pompous theme that had to be "grandiose in style, symbolizing the entry through the gates into London."[22] The piece matches the celebratory remarks of the Wordsworth-quoting Minister of Health, whose glorious speech about the clean city is interrupted by the sight of a naked female body floating in the Thames. Goodwin's music is thus the perfect counterpoint to this surprising twist, unlike Mancini's cue, which lent London a grim and Gothic aura, foreshadowing the coming of a second Jack the Ripper. The medieval feeling is mostly established through a gloomy organ solo, although this seemingly dominant instrument will not be utilized in the rest of the score at all.

As in all of his recordings, Mancini made several changes on his re-recorded "Frenzy" theme, which has led to misunderstandings about the original sound. For instance, the theme's original recording (briefly heard in the documentary *The Story of Frenzy*) is much slower and the main instrument is an extremely deep and morose church organ.[23] Another small change is that Mancini recorded the

Figure 1. The first measures of the unrecorded organ solo at the beginning of "Main Title." Instructions to Mancini's assistant frequently appear in the cue sheets.

shorter version of the cue, but the "Main Title" originally had two beginnings. The first seven measures were written for an organ solo, accompanied by some strings (barely heard in the recording) at the end (fig. 1), providing an ominous opening to what may have been timed to the usually unscored Universal logo. It is unknown whether Mancini recorded this opening during the original London session, but he definitely didn't include it in his 1990 re-recording for *Mancini in Surround*. This is not too surprising, since this collection was designed as a pleasant listening experience of previously unavailable Mancini pieces, and the extended solo took away from the cue's powerful second opening.

2. *My Tie Is Your Tie [M-102]*

1:09, 20 measures. Orchestration: 4 Bass Flutes, 4 Bass Clarinets, 4 Bassoons, 4 French Horns, 8 Violas, 8 Celli, 6 Basses, 2 Harps

This cue highlights the first great deviation from the music in Hitchcock's final version of the movie, because it underscores a sequence that had no music in the finished cut. "My Tie Is Your Tie" was written for the discovery of the naked body in the Thames, highlighting the gloomy tone of the score quite early on. Mancini generally used a lot of bass woodwinds in his score and this may have been one of the reasons Hitchcock disliked it. (The same bass flutes providing dark colors in this score played a vital role in Bernard Herrmann's eventually unused *Torn Curtain* score as well.) Mancini only made note of two important synch points to which he had to time the changes in his music: a close-up of the girl's body with a tie around her neck and a cut to Blaney in his room, just putting the finishing touches on a very similar tie. A new thematic element introduced in this cue involves an overarching theme for the murders with a heavy hit underscoring the transition to Blaney and effectively making him the suspect through the music. The cue's title itself is a play on this idea, highlighting a red herring. This is one of the few cues with a date indicating when it was completed: 20 November 1971.

3. *Posh For Two* [M-301]

2:48, 57 measures. Orchestration: Solo Violin, Solo Cello, Solo Piano

This source music, written for an ensemble of three instruments, would have been heard during Blaney's reconciliatory dinner with Brenda in a fancy restaurant. The music was recorded wild and contains no synch points in the sketches. While basically a throwaway piece of background music, it lends a slightly different feel to the scene when compared with Goodwin's similarly orchestrated cue. The latter composition evokes a sense of melancholy and heavy-handed nostalgia as the couple recounts their past mistakes. Mancini's music on the other hand is more light-hearted. As indicated by the title, it is a posh waltz, which makes the restaurant seem even a bit fancier. This different composition evokes a sense of more spirited nostalgia, focusing on the good times of Blaney and Brenda, leading into their peaceful settlement, which eventually results in the husband becoming the prime suspect in the woman's sadistic murder.

4. My Kind of Woman [M-302/400]

3:06, 28 measures. Orchestration: 2 Harps, Piano, 4 Bass Flutes, 4 Bass Clarinets, 2 Bassoon, 4 French Horns, Violas, Celli, Basses

This is another section that Hitchcock ultimately left without music, yet Mancini wrote one of his longest cues for the sequence starting just after Rusk says "I love you" to Brenda. Mancini's title slightly revises a subsequent key line—"You're my type of woman"—and the cue uses the murder theme in a carefully constructed piece that slowly builds tension. Audience members may realize that Rusk is the necktie killer at different points in the awkward conversation, but Mancini's spotting would have synchronized this realization with the start of the music. An eerie subdued harp and piano melody begins this cue, which lasts until Brenda tries to pick up the phone and call for help. At this point, the bass woodwinds are introduced, recalling the melody that we could hear in "My Tie Is Your Tie." Finally the strings enter when, according to Mancini's notes, Brenda is "against the wall." The music builds to a crescendo as Rusk throws her on the table, ending the music when "she faints." The date that this cue was completed is noted as 21 November 1971.

Hitchcock was always quite choosy in scoring his murder scenes. He famously wanted no music under the shower scene of *Psycho,* and the killing of Stasi agent Gromek was a focal point of discord between him and his composers in *Torn Curtain.* While both Bernard Herrmann and his replacement composer John Addison wrote music for the scene where Michael Armstrong fights and kills Gromek, Hitchcock eventually decided to play that scene without music. This was done to emphasize the realism of the scene and highlight how incredibly difficult and disturbing it is to kill a man (as opposed to the quick and easy killings shown in most contemporary movies). The scene with Rusk and Brenda has similar

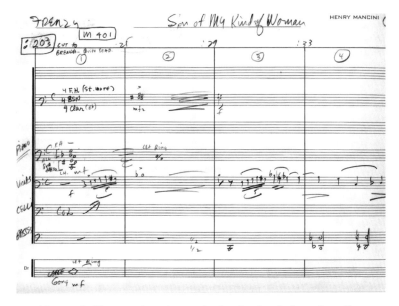

Figure 2. The synch point at the beginning helps place the cue correctly within the lengthy scene of Brenda's murder.

dynamics, enhanced by the lack of music for the lead-up to the rape scene. While Mancini himself left the actual murder unscored as well, he wanted to frame the shocking sequence with two interrelated cues. Hitchcock obviously thought that only the murder's aftermath needed musical accompaniment.

5. Son of My Kind of Woman [M-401]

2:29, 34 measures. Orchestration: 4 French Horns, 4 Bass Flutes (Double Alto Flute), 4 Bassoon, 4 Clarinets (Double Bass Clarinet), Piano, Violas, Celli, Basses, 2 Harps

This is Mancini's composition for the aftermath of Rusk's murder, beginning with a "cut to Brenda, quite dead." The music again begins with a dissonant piano hit (fig. 2). Something similar happens in "My Tie Is Your Tie" when the film cuts to Blaney and his tie. This simple motif seems to become a calling card of the necktie murderer, which is most often used during the shocking revelatory shot of Rusk's new victims. Goodwin's replacement score starts the music at the exact same place and uses an even more exaggerated crescendo to communicate the horrors brought on by the killer. Mancini's composition includes several synch points, such as Blaney's appearance or his saying "Hello" at Brenda's door, at which point the bass flutes make their entrance. Yet the biggest difference between the two scores is how they handle the arrival of the secretary. In Mancini's work, a simple repetitive thumping of the piano follows the woman's steps, after Blaney has already left the premises. Goodwin stops the music at the moment when the secretary entering the building goes through the door. There's a lengthy static shot of the building with only the street noise being heard until the secretary screams upon the discovery of her boss. Mancini's piano theme would have played until the actual scream. The change in spotting created a recognizable Hitchcock moment with great silence preceding a shocking event.

The title of this cue may need some explanation. This kind of wordplay was consistent in Mancini's body of work when he wanted to indicate that a given cue is a strict thematic continuation of a previous composition. The lengthy finale of the Cannon horror film *Lifeforce* (1985) was scored with three long cues, simply titled "Web of Destiny," "Son of Web," and "Grandson of Web." Compared to this, "Son of My Kind of Woman" is a restrained pun. According to the logs, this cue was finished on 22 November 1971.

6. Exit Oscar Wilde [M-501/600]

2:37, 46 measures. Orchestration: 2 Harps, Violins, Celli, Basses, 4 French Horns, 4 Bassoon, Piano, Vibraphone, 4 Alto Flutes, 4 Bass Clarinets

This is one of the few cues where the spotting didn't change between Mancini's and Goodwin's cues, although the pieces have different dynamics. The title refers to the fake name Blaney gave at a hotel he went to with Babs. The cue would have begun with a shot of a newspaper announcing another necktie murder. The music underscores the hotel staff's realization that "Oscar Wilde" may be the killer. They call the police, who break into the rented suite, only to find an "empty room" (Mancini's only synch point in this cue). Goodwin's music is more energetic and becomes almost frantic when the policemen break into the hotel room. Mancini's cue, on the other hand, conveys slowly escalating terror, adding new instruments only when the manager runs out the door to fetch the policemen. Both cues have an effective coda to underscore the surprise revelation of the empty hotel room, but while Goodwin's solution is a major crescendo, Mancini employs the same piano hit that played during the first shot of Brenda's dead body in "Son of My Kind of Woman."

7. Big Drag For Babs [M-701]

0:59, 16 bars. Orchestration: Violins, Celli, Basses, Piano, 4 Alto Flutes, 4 Bassoon, 4 French Horns, 4 Bass Clarinets

By far the most unnecessary of Mancini's cues was originally intended to underscore a scene where Hitchcock eventually decided to utilize an exciting sound experiment instead of music (hence Goodwin never wrote music for this section). This one-minute long cue would have covered the memorable shot after Rusk and Babs enter a room, preceded by his saying "You're my type of woman" (the same thing he said before murdering Brenda). Mancini underscored this statement with the fateful piano note, then reprised the extended murder theme (originally heard in "My Tie Is Your Tie") for the shot where the camera is backing out of the apartment building in one single take. Even if Mancini's score had been used, it is very unlikely that the director would have kept this piece in the film. Hitchcock's final notes on the sound design of *Frenzy* go into more detail on the role of sound effects for this scene, deliberately emphasizing and overplaying the street noise in order to drown out Babs's call for help.[24] Mancini's recording for this scene would have considerably lessened the impact of the lengthy silent shot, and it could also have drowned out the street noise, which was only added at the very last stage and was never designed together with any kind of music.

8. Hot Potatos [sic] [M-801]

2:01, 28 measures. Orchestration: 2 Harps, Violins, Celli, Basses, 4 Bass Flutes, 4 Bassoon, French Horns, 4 Bass Clarinets

Another mysterioso cue is played when Rusk disposes of Babs's body, placing it in a potato truck. Once again, the spotting is significantly different from Hitchcock's finished version. Mancini's music begins when Rusk tows the body out on a wheelbarrow and continues as he tosses it into the potatoes. The music uses mostly deep strings and bass woodwinds to convey the sense of menace, then switches into a more relaxed mode when Babs is buried in the truck. Goodwin's music only enters at this point, once Rusk has dispatched the body and throws away the cap that was a part of his disguise. Again, Hitchcock wanted to leave the scene of death unscored, providing a deliciously twisted soundscape through neutral sound effects and the annoyingly squeaky wheelbarrow. Despite the difference in how they begin, both cues end at the same time as Rusk enters his apartment and the scene shifts to Chief Inspector Oxford, who is still baffled by the case.

9. Babs Grabs [M-802]

1:19, 49 bars. Orchestration: 4 French Horns, 4 Bass Flutes, 4 Bassoons, 4 Clarinets (Double Bass Clarinet), Violins, Violas, Celli, Basses, Piano

Finally here's a scene that Mancini and Goodwin approached in a similar manner (fig. 3). Rusk's flashback to the murder and losing his pin is underscored with a hurried

Figure 3. The entire sequence for "Babs Grabs" now memorably plays in silence as the camera rolls out on the street in a long, unedited shot.

version of the murder theme. Then Mancini provides some twisted atonal material as the killer runs towards the potato truck to get rid of the damning evidence. This is one sequence that relies heavily on the music in both versions. Mancini even explicitly marked the bits of dialogue to which his music reacted. Hearing the words "See you later!" from the truck driver increases Rusk's panic, which is reflected in the last few bars of music that then suddenly stops with the slamming of the car door. While the darkly comic sequence of Rusk throwing around potato bags to get to his victim is unscored in both versions, the two composers bid farewell to the listener in different ways. Mancini timed his last note to coincide with the sound of the car door slamming. Goodwin wrote a bit more music to finish his contribution in a more subdued manner. His cue ends just a few seconds after Mancini's, unglamorously fading out with the burst of the engine noise.

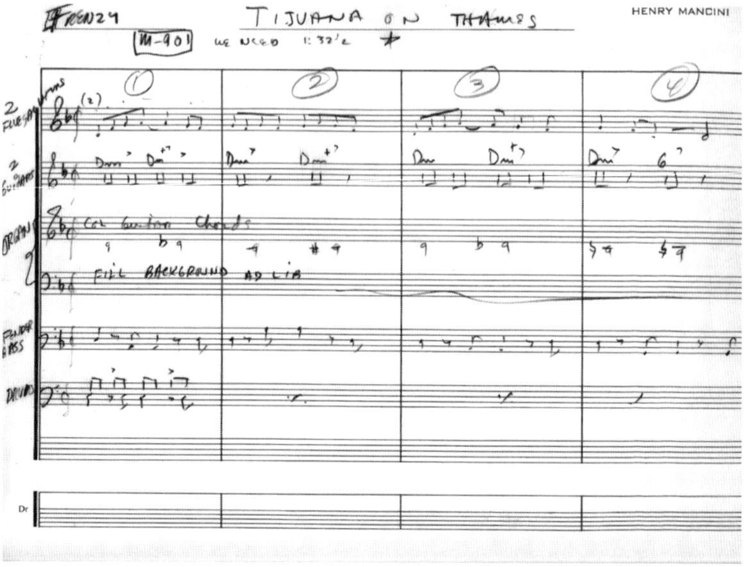

Figure 4. "Tijuana on Thames" was one of the two source cues written for the film. It relied largely on improvisation.

10. *Tijuana on Thames [M-901]*

1:32, 37 measures. Orchestration: 2 Flugelhorns, 2 Guitars, Organ, Fender Bass, Drums

Alongside "Posh For Two," "Tijuana on Thames" may be the most typical Mancini composition of the entire soundtrack (fig. 4). Appearing as source music from a café as Rusk climbs off the potato truck, this bit was written wild and was meant to be recorded with a smaller ensemble. While "Posh For Two" utilized only three musicians from the original orchestra, this piece needed some drums and a Fender bass, which had to be contracted separately. Since source music is usually recorded separately from the rest of the score because of the different number of players, it is unclear whether Mancini got around to actually recording "Tijuana on Thames."

Mancini's sketch is very light for this cue, only laying out the basics and allowing for many free improvisations by the soloists. Although the composer wrote a proper coda for the piece, most source cues just simply die out when the scene shifts to another location. Hence even if it was recorded, it is very unlikely that the finale would have been used. There's not much difference between "Tijuana on Thames" and Goodwin's composition for the same scene. Perhaps Mancini's is more old-fashioned than the mod-sounding cue from the replacement score, but otherwise both tracks are unrelated to the main score and are merely functional in providing a sleazy atmosphere in the café that Rusk peeks into after his nighttime escapade.

11. The Inspector Thinks [M-1001]

0:46, 12 bars. Orchestration: 2 Harps, Piano, Violas, Celli, Basses, Timpani

This cue is the only place where material from the "Main Title" returns, and again it is written for a scene where Goodwin provided no underscore. As in the case of "Big Drag For Babs," Mancini's score would have clashed with one of Hitchcock's favorite audio games. The gloomy music would have begun with Blaney being thrown into jail, but the scene then cuts to Chief Inspector Oxford, who remains in the courtroom and thinks about what he just heard.

In this sequence, Hitchcock plays sound bites from Blaney's rant after his conviction, showing the policeman reviewing the information and looking around nervously. The sound bites were already part of Mancini's work print, since a quote of the monologue ("Rusk did it!") is one of the synch points. The music grows more and more nervous as the inspector realizes his mistake, but the musical representation of his thoughts was deemed unnecessary by Hitchcock. The powerful conclusion would have already clashed with the sound bites, hence the director stood by the more innovative solution and didn't have a cue written for the scene when the score was rewritten.

12. Rusk on Candid Camera [M-1101]

0:18, 7 bars. Orchestration: 4 Bass Flutes, 4 Bassoons, 4 Bass Clarinets, 2 Harps, Piano, Vibraphone

This very brief cue appears immediately after a reel change and the maddening conclusion of "The Inspector Thinks." It has no counterpart in Goodwin's score. The cue was written for a short sequence when the Inspector travels to Rusk's shop and asks his partner to take a mug shot of him which he can show to Brenda's secretary. The music plays as a sort of upbeat version of the material heard during the murders, and accompanies imagery of the serial killer minding his own business on a regular day. The cue once again ends with an ominous piano hit on a "cut to photo of Rusk" (per Mancini's own note).

13. Off to Rusk's Place [M-1201]

4:10, 65 bars. Orchestration: Solo Bass, Solo Cello, Solo Viola, 4 Bass Flutes, 2 Harps, Violas, 4 Bassoons, 4 Bass Clarinet, Vibraphone, Timpani, Piano, 4 French Horns

The longest of Mancini's cues was written for a scene that was spotted exactly the same way in Goodwin's version. The music covers Blaney's escape from the hospital and his trip to Rusk's flat. Mancini's only scene-specific synch point was adding a bit of dialogue ("sleeping pills") over his sketch (fig. 5), but his cue is more or less in synch with the entire sequence. The moody opening passage underscores the nighttime conspiracy, providing a hint of suspense over Blaney's dialogue with another patient. The score changes pace with the aforementioned discovery. Blaney's drive to his former friend's place is underscored with the most action-driven segment of the entire score. Thumping percussion with maniacal undertones follow the vengeful convict. As in Goodwin's score, the music would have ended with the arrival at Rusk's flat. Yet even this most forceful section of the

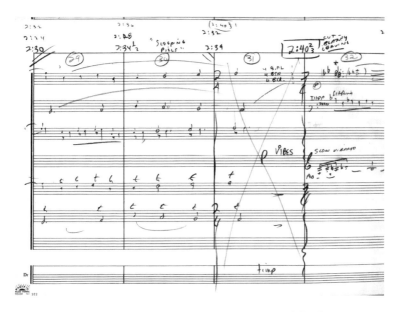

Figure 5. This section of "Off to Rusk's Place is full of timing notes at the top of the page.

underscore is quite tame when compared with Hitchcock's final choice. It is interesting to note that the next scene (Blaney's entrance to Rusk's flat) was left unscored in Mancini's version, providing another striking contrast to Goodwin's version. While Hitchcock usually left out cues for scenes that Mancini already scored, in this case he wanted more music for his finale.

14. End Credits/End Rusk [M-1202]

0:40, 14 bars. Orchestration: 4 Alto Flutes, 4 Bassoons, 4 French Horns, 4 Bass Clarinets, 1 Harp, Violas, Celli, Basses

Although it is not strictly part of the narrative (since no action happens on the screen), the end credits of every score are very important from a dramatic point of view. It is particularly interesting to compare the two end credits of

Figure 6. Mancini's "End Credits" closes the movie on a more reflective note than Goodwin's cue for the same sequence.

Frenzy. Hitchcock's own notes reveal that he originally wanted romantic music by Goodwin to be played in this scene, but this material was never written. The director instead opted to feature a reprise of the grim *Frenzy* theme over the closing shot. While Goodwin's music reinforces the theme of vengeance, Mancini wrote a cue that highlights Hitchcock's original, romantic vision (fig. 6). A darkly melancholic love theme (which had no predecessor in the score) offers a more subdued conclusion for the movie. Mancini closed his sketch with the acronym "E.O.P." (End of Picture) over the fourteenth bar of the only unused score of his career.

Conclusion

What can we make of the rejection of Henry Mancini's *Frenzy*? While Ron Goodwin had the chance to work from explicitly written instructions, Mancini didn't have this luxury. Considering that Hitchcock went against many of the basic ideas of the original score, it seems that either he was unsure of his own approach when the first composer was hired, or he only realized his mistakes during the recording process. The nature of the perceived mistakes was never clarified in any of Hitchcock's own interviews: for example, did the bass woodwinds remind the director of Herrmann's *Torn Curtain*? Or did he really just want more upbeat music that juxtaposed the darkness instead of emphasizing it through its uncompromising atonal soundscape? Unfortunately, wistful speculation will never answer these questions.

What we can gather from an examination of the two scores is that Hitchcock significantly revised his own stance on the music. Mancini scored several scenes around the murders that the director eventually left without music. How to use music in death sequences has always been a central question in Hitchcock's works, where some murders are played out in silence (such as the death of Gromek in *Torn Curtain*) and others are expertly spotted musical sequences (such as the shower murder in *Psycho*). Mancini's treatment of *Frenzy* leans towards the latter approach, while Hitchcock's final decision was apparently to lean toward the former. This is all the more evident if we look at the moments that were spotted differently: the scenes that would have been covered by "My Tie Is Your Time," "My Kind of Woman," "Big Drag For Babs," "The Inspector Thinks," and "Rusk on Candid Camera" didn't have any underscore, and "Son of My Kind of Woman" and "Hot Potatos" were also significantly reworked in terms of spotting. These cues reveal that Mancini's score mostly focused on scenes depicting Rusk or his murders, while Goodwin's music covered more sequences with Blaney in the spotlight.

Even if Hitchcock had used Mancini's music, he would have omitted more than half of the written cues, thus leading to a compromised score. Some of *Frenzy*'s best-known scenes play well without music, and these special moments (such as the camera pulling back from the apartment and the death scream of Babs being obliterated by overplayed traffic noise) would be less effective with any kind of score played over them. It seems that instead of radically re-editing Mancini's music, Hitchcock opted to start a completely new collaboration with different ground rules and a new concept from which he didn't need to cut a second (a rare feat on any kind of score). It is perhaps preferable that we get to have one complete Ron Goodwin score instead of a drastically abbreviated Mancini one from which over half the cues would have been left out. The notion of rejecting an entire score may seem hurtful to collectors of film music and especially to the composer who is involved, but a good director is only interested in the combined effectiveness of the music and the film. This is what Hitchcock excelled at, even if he had to make painful decisions at times to achieve his ultimate goal, sacrificing Mancini's very interesting compositions in order to allow for the creation of what Peter Bogdanovich later claimed was the best of the non-Herrmann scores, one more suited to Hitchcock's overall cinematic intentions in *Frenzy*.[25]

Notes

Special thanks to Christian Téxier, whose knowledge helped me understand the music much better. The images reproduced in my essay appear courtesy of the estate of Henry Mancini.

   1. Quoted in Jack Sullivan, *Hitchcock's Music* (New Haven: Yale University Press, 2006), 312-13.
   2. Since moving to Hollywood, the only Hitchcock score to be (partially) recorded in London was *Vertigo*, which doesn't fit any of the other details in the quotation, hence my deduction that the director was talking about *Frenzy*.
   3. Sullivan, *Hitchcock's Music*, 298—307.
   4. Allusions to Herrmann's *Torn Curtain* can be heard in the following cues: "The Turning Point" (*Battle of Neretva*), "Idea" (*Airplane!*), and "The Fight" (*Cape Fear*).
   5. Michael Schelle, *The Score* (Los Angeles: Silman-James Press, 1999), 388.

6. Sullivan preempts undue speculation about the rejected score by indicating in an endnote that "My attempts to get information from Mancini's surviving colleagues proved fruitless" (*Hitchcock's Music*, 336).

7. As Mancini himself put it: "Memory was fresher then, and I can do no better than to quote—with Tony's permission—what I told him then." Henry Mancini, *Did They Mention the Music?* (New York: Cooper Square Press, 2001), 155.

8. Mancini, *Did They Mention the Music?*, 60.

9. Sullivan, *Hitchcock's Music*, 299.

10. Mancini, *Did They Mention the Music?*, 155-56.

11. In an interview with author (not composer) John Williams, Ron Goodwin famously said about this replacement: "Poor old William Walton being replaced by this unknown composer. I mean what about poor old Ron Goodwin?" Goodwin's career was apparently affected by his decision to replace one of Britain's leading composers. See *From Silents to Satellites* 1, nos. 1-2 (February/May, 1990).

12. Selections of the notes can be seen in *The Story of* Frenzy, Laurent Bouzereau's behind-the scenes documentary from 2001 dvd. Other selections are available in Sullivan, *Hitchcock's Music*, 298-307.

13. Mancini, *Did They Mention the Music?*, 156.

14. Sullivan, *Hitchcock's Music*, 298.

15. Quoted in Donald Spoto: *The Dark Side of Genius: The Life of Alfred Hitchcock* (New York: Da Capo Press, 1999), 515.

16. Leslie T. Zador and Gregory Rose, "A Conversation with Bernard Herrmann," in *Film Music I*, ed. Clifford McCarthy (Los Angeles: The Film Music Society, 1998), 243. For Jarre's response, see Zador and Rose, "Conversation," 252.

17. Herrmann's comment was "I am not a pop composer . . . get a pop composer"; quoted in Zador and Rose, "Conversation," 219.

18. Mancini, *Did They Mention the Music?*, 156.

19. The sketches used were the basis of the fully orchestrated score, which didn't seem to survive. As such, the reconstructions themselves are skeletal, but still have perfect timings, which was the primary focus in this project.

20. The original sketches only contained hard-to-read abbreviations. Luckily the separate document was already scanned and contained Mancini's intended line-up of the orchestra.

21. One or two timing marks appeared on every page. The synch points were jotted at the top of the pages, which made it easy to calculate the exact beginning of the cue.

22. Hitchcock's notes on the soundtrack of *Frenzy*, quoted in Sullivan, *Hitchcock's Music*, 300.

23. *The Story of* Frenzy.

24. Hitchcock's notes are quoted in detail in Sullivan, *Hitchcock's Music*, 304.

25. Bogdanovich makes this comment in *The Story of* Frenzy.

JAMES NAREMORE

Hitchcock Now

Thomas Leitch and Leland Poague, eds., *A Companion to Alfred Hitchcock*. Malden, MA: Wiley-Blackwell, 2011.

David Boyd and R. Barton Palmer, eds., *Hitchcock at the Source: The Auteur as Adapter*. Albany: State University of New York Press, 2011.

The history of writing on Alfred Hitchcock since the 1950s, like the history of film studies more generally, can be divided into three overlapping phases, two of which are marked by sporadic internal divisions or conflicts. The initial phase, ending in the early to mid-1970s, was the moment of high auteurism, when Hitchcock's reputation as a major artist was secured. This was the period of Eric Rohmer and Claude Chabrol's *Hitchcock: The First Forty-Four Films* (1957 in France, 1979 in the U.S.), the first edition of Robin Wood's *Hitchcock's Films* (1965), François Truffaut's interview book (1967), and Andrew Sarris's *The American Cinema* (1968). The Hitchcockians were triumphant, but there were important dissenting voices, including Georges Sadoul and André Bazin in France and Raymond Durgnat in England, who questioned the degree to which Hitchcock should be regarded as a serious artist. (These arguments were much more intense in some quarters; it's difficult for young people today to appreciate just how outrageous it seemed to the 1960s establishment when Hitchcock's admirers described him as a better director than Ingmar Bergman.) Durgnat's *The*

Strange Case of Alfred Hitchcock (1974), conceived in part as a rejoinder to Robin Wood, became a strange case itself. Although it lacked the rhetorical power of Wood's book, it was more comprehensive, more aware of the merits of Hitchcock's British work, and more attuned to such things as politics, sexual psychology, and the business of film production; nevertheless, it was neglected in academia and is seldom mentioned by contemporary writers on Hitchcock—perhaps because it casts doubt on Hitchcock's "genius" and finds many of his Hollywood films too slick and commercially calculated. In Durgnat's words, "Hitchcock has always been an entertainer whose work can, on occasion, and for one reason or another, reach a degree of sophistication and intensity such that his material takes on sufficient truth, urgency and challenge to qualify as a significant artist (and whether he's a minor or major one is another matter again; but to be a minor artist is no mean achievement)."

The second phase, beginning around 1968 in France and continuing elsewhere throughout the 1980s, was the moment of feminism and various critiques of ideology, which were lumped together under the rubric of Theory. The period was typified by the writings of Michel Foucault and Roland Barthes against the idea of the author; Jean-Louis Baudry's attack on the "cinematic apparatus"; Laura Mulvey's analysis of the sadistic/fetishistic male gaze in *Vertigo, Rear Window,* and *Marnie*; Raymond Bellour's semiotic-psychoanalytic investigation of key Hitchcock films and sequences; and Stephen Heath's deconstruction of classic narrative space in *Suspicion*. A residual auteurism persisted, as in books on Hitchcock by William Rothman, Elizabeth Weis, and Maurice Yacowar; but elsewhere "Hitchcock" was increasingly treated as a "name-of-the-author" that had been created by an ideologically pernicious system. Certain books split the difference between the two schools: theoretical and auteurist, they emphasized questions of ideology but were complex or divided in their judgments of Hitchcock. The 1977 edition of Wood's *Hitchcock's Films* grew out of Wood's criticism of his own earlier work, which had been influenced by F.R. Leavis and also had something in common with Lionel Trilling's "moral realism." Wood now lamented Hitchcock's tendency to view "bourgeois normality as empty and unsatisfying and everything beyond it as terrifying." By the end of the decade, having acknowledged his homosexuality and become interested in psychoanalysis and Marxism, he was writing penetrating analysis of such films as *Shadow of a Doubt* and *Blackmail*, revealing both their artistic and ideological dimensions. At roughly the same time, Tania Modleski's *The Women Who Knew Too Much: Hitchcock and Feminist Film Theory* (1988) took a position counter to Laura Mulvey, viewing Hitchcock as a filmmaker who encouraged "identification with femininity" but whose implicit attitude toward women oscillated between sympathy and misogyny. Finally, Slavoj Žižek turned the tables, reading Lacan in terms of Hitchcock. Žižek's anthology, *Everything You Always Wanted to Know about Lacan but were Afraid to Ask Hitchcock*, published in France in 1988 but not translated into English until 1992, was a *tour de force* of ideological interpretation that made the auteur safe for Theory.

The third stage, where we are now, might be called the age of the Hitchcock industry, a period of a remarkable growth in the number of essays, books, and anthologies on Hitchcock. (The 1995 edition of Jane E. Sloan's annotated Hitchcock filmography has 1,042 entries covering the years between 1919 and 1994, but there was a massive surge of publication over the next seventeen years.) Intelligent journalistic criticism, at least in the United States, has been hampered by the decline in the number and quality of newspapers and the concomitant rise of relatively casual Internet blogging, and serious scholarship and criticism are now confined almost entirely to the academic sphere. Within the academy, the humanities have moved away from Theory and toward historical and cultural studies—Robert Kapsis's *Hitchcock: the Making of a Reputation* (1992) is symptomatic of the trend. Given this environment, the academic study of authorship has a low priority, and yet it sometimes seems as if almost everybody who professes film has had something to say about Hitchcock. In the English-speaking world, Richard Allen, Sidney Gottlieb, and Ken Mogg have helped to create a large and lively community of interest in the great director. The period has produced the splendid Hitchcock centenary at NYU, a collection of centenary essays, and the journal you are now reading—and also the two excellent volumes under review here, which by my count involve fifty almost entirely new essays by forty-four different contributors.

Along with several others, I've already expressed my admiration for *A Companion to Alfred Hitchcock* in a short blurb on the back cover, where I praise the book as a wide-ranging, consistently intelligent compendium that proves there are plenty of new things to say about Hitchcock. By virtue of its size and scope, the *Companion* also enables me to make generalizations about the present moment. It would appear that among the signal characteristics of the age of the Hitchcock industry, in contrast with the two previous periods, are catholicity—the editors of the *Companion* make exactly this play on words—and a tendency to smooth over any feeling that one school of thought is dominant over others. Many of the essays in this volume have an almost sacerdotal respect for the director, and when the editors call attention to disagreements, they don't take sides.

Of course a project of this sort needs to try to provide a place for everybody—as long as they take Hitchcock seriously. (It's appropriate that the book is dedicated to Robin Wood and contains a useful essay on Wood by Harry Oldmeadow.) There are sections on Hitchcock's historical background, on genre, on collaboration, on style, on career development, on auteurism, on ideology, on "ethics" (covering not only ethical but also religious, psychological, and philosophical issues), and on "beyond," which deals with Hitchcock's legacy and relation to postmodernity. The editors confess to having arranged some of the contributions in ways that "foster implicit controversy," but the controversy never seems radically significant. There's no evidence of a newly emerging critical or theoretical paradigm, and whatever differences one might notice among critics are allowed to remain differences. Was Hitchcock a romantic, a Victorian, a modernist, a postmodernist, or all of the above? Was he conservative or subversive? Was his approach to cinema influenced more by England or Hollywood? Does his style owe more to theater or prose fiction? Were his films determined by his personal vision or by collaboration? Did he hate women and homosexuals or identify with them? Was he actively engaged in dramatizing ethical and moral conflict or was he shaped by the prevailing ideological currents? You will find nuanced statements on nearly all these positions in the various essays, and the volume ends in irenic style with an eloquent essay by Richard Allen, who views Hitchcock in double-edged fashion as a romantic ironist, emphasizing that he should be interpreted in both/and rather than either/or terms.

No collection of essays on Hitchcock can ever be complete in what it covers, but this one is impressively designed to touch on almost everything. Close readings of individual films were discouraged by the editors, a strategy that pays off handsomely when many of the contributors, including Thomas Hemmeter, Paula Marantz Cohen, Brigitte Peucker, Murray Pomerance, Richard Gilmore, and Todd McGowan, seize on an aspect of Hitchcock's work and make arguments for its systemic importance. The longest section of the book, containing essays by Sidney Gottlieb, Tom Ryall, Ina Rae Hark, David Sterritt, Joe McElhaney, and William Rothman, could have been published as a self-contained monograph filled with valuable historical information and critical observation about the different historical phases of Hitchcock's career. To my mind, the most important thing missing from all this wealth of commentary—an absence that made me wonder if we're taking Hitchcock *too* seriously—is greater attention to wit and humor. In their introduction, the editors express regret for the lack of commentary on comedy; but we do have Lesley Brill's essay on "Hitchcock's Romance," which, like his earlier book on

Hitchcock, calls attention to Northrop Frye's ur-generic *mythoi* and enables us to distinguish between Hitchcock's romantic comedy and romantic tragedy. What doesn't get enough emphasis are the pleasurable air of glamour in certain of the films and the sometimes playful, sometimes troubling atmosphere of dark humor, jokes, and pranks (as opposed to comedy, irony, or satire) that permeates most of Hitchcock's work and almost defines his public persona. (One of the places where such things are very strongly evident is in Hitchcock's TV films—about which, except for Richard R. Ness's remarks on the melodramatic qualities of "Incident at a Corner," the *Companion* has unfortunately little to say.)

Throughout, the standard of criticism and scholarship in the volume is consistently high, and I noticed very few proofreading slips for such a large tome (one minor glitch is that some of the contributors refer to their work as "this chapter" and others as "this essay"). Different readers will find different essays especially useful, so rather than handing out prizes I'll simply point to a handful of items that were of particular interest for me. On the scholarly side, Charles Barr's discussion of early filmmakers and their influence on Hitchcock is wonderfully informative—as is James M. Vest's account of the French reception of Hitchcock in the decade after World War II, parts of which were previously published in his book on the subject and in the *Hitchcock Annual*. Also where the French are concerned, Janet Bergstrom, who is well qualified for the job, had the simple, excellent idea of listening to the entire tape-recorded Truffaut-Hitchcock interview and comparing it to what was published in Truffaut's condensed, highly edited book. The omissions and changes aren't terribly scandalous; for example, in their conversations Hitchcock mentioned some names that he didn't want to be published, and made critical remarks about various people, including Truffaut's other hero, Jean Renoir. One of the many nice details that didn't make it onto the page is when he tells Truffaut that *The Birds* will have "silence made of sound." These recordings obviously have great intrinsic value and Bergstrom is right to argue that they ought to be made available to scholars in a digital form.

On the side of criticism and theory, Joe McElhaney's discussion of Hitchcock at Paramount offers a beautifully detailed analysis of cinematic *mise-en-scène*, a concept that too few critics have properly understood. In my view, his essay should be recommended to students at every level. I have the same enthusiasm for Alexander Doty's "Queer Hitchcock," which is not only a well-informed account of Hitchcock's films but also an efficient theoretical house-cleaning that shows how normative standards of gender and sexuality are always unstable and changing, and how "queer" can describe such a range of things that it seems paradoxically natural. Finally, Tania Modleski, in the course of a fine essay on Hitchcock's many female collaborators, is almost unique among the contributors in reminding us of a crucial point: most critics of Hitchcock could be regarded as collaborators with the ideological effects of the films, because critical interpretation produces meanings and helps to canonize the director; but one of the purposes of good criticism might be to join, at least to some degree, with the forces of resistance, not so much by attacking Hitchcock but by developing what Paul Ricoeur called "a hermeneutics of suspicion."

The second of the two collections under review, *Hitchcock at the Source: The Adapter as Auteur*, could be viewed as something of a bookend to editors R. Barton Palmer and David Boyd's earlier anthology, *After Hitchcock: Influence, Imitation, and Intertextuality* (2006), and is more obviously representative of certain general tendencies in contemporary film studies. Its twenty essays have been prompted by the new wave of interest in cinematic adaptation, which in the past twelve years has produced at least six books and four anthologies on the subject in English, plus an academic periodical entitled *Adaptation*.

Hitchcock might seem an improbable topic for a project of this kind. The great majority of his films have sources in prose fiction or theater (and in one case a nonfiction magazine article), and at one point he even considered a modernized version of *Hamlet* starring Cary Grant; but despite what Palmer, Boyd, and some essayists in the collection occasionally seem to suggest, relatively few of his films could be described as pure adaptations, or as what Julie Sanders, in *Adaptation and Appropriation* (2006), has described as "sustained engagement with a single text or source." Furthermore, as Palmer and Boyd point out, few of the films were rhetorically positioned or marketed as adaptations, even when they stayed reasonably close to the narratives of successful plays such as *Rope* or well-known novels such as *The Thirty-Nine Steps*. Only twice in his American career did Hitchcock adapt best-selling novels with "pre-sold" reputations that required him to foreground the source and remain true to what readers expected: the first was Daphne du Maurier's *Rebecca*, which he tried to alter considerably before being reined in by David Selznick, and the second was Leon Uris's *Topaz*, which many of his fans have underrated because it doesn't seem enough like *The 39 Steps* or *North by Northwest*. Otherwise, Hitchcock was a proponent of what he liked to call "pure cinema" and a careful manager of his image or brand who tried to avoid being associated with literary adaptation. He may have respected some of his writers (see his extravagant tribute to Thornton Wilder in the credits of *Shadow of a Doubt*) but he always saw to it that they worked under his personal command and control (hence Raymond Chandler's frustration and anger during the preparation of *Strangers on a Train*). Although he took material from such figures as Joseph Conrad, Noël Coward, Patricia Highsmith, Sean O'Casey, John Galsworthy, and Somerset Maugham, he tended to play down the origins of his films and often made very basic changes when he appropriated texts. Some of his earliest pictures were derived from authors who were famous at the time but soon drifted into obscurity: we remain interested in Hitchcock, but how many among us have read or care to read Eden Philpotts? By the same token, some of Hitchcock's celebrated Hollywood films were inspired by pulp fiction, slick magazine stories or crime novels that had relatively little recognition in their own day and are now virtually forgotten.

As *Hitchcock at the Source* demonstrates, however, the study of the fiction and theater that prompted Hitchcock's films reveals a great deal about his working methods and the changing cultural environment of his long career. Some of the contributors debunk the straw-man notion of the films as purely original conceptions that simply popped out of his head (even the most vulgar auteurists haven't claimed that) and now and then one of the essays overstates similarities between a film and its source. In his otherwise helpful discussion of *Psycho*, for example, Brian McFarlane argues that what distinguishes the film from the Robert Bloch novel is "not so much the events that make up the narrative" as the "different semiotic system" in which the events are told. But in fact the film makes dozens of major changes that have nothing to do with cinema-specific codes: it elaborates the Marion Crane story into a full-scale double plot, shifts the location, alters the interior settings, rewrites the dialogue, creates new characters, makes basic revisions within scenes, and completely transforms the characterization of Marion and Norman. (If a film took these liberties with a Jane Austen novel, we probably wouldn't call it an adaptation.) When the essays are less concerned with questions of fidelity they tend to produce better results, as when R. Barton Palmer examines *Secret Agent* in relation to Maugham and the larger history of spy fiction, or when Thomas Leitch contributes a brilliant overview of Hitchcock and adaptation that asks whether the films were more indebted to theater or prose fiction. Leitch's answer, contrary to what many critics might think, is that Hitchcock has more in common with the page than with the stage; Leitch then goes on to make extremely interesting comparisons between free-indirect narration in Hitchcock's sources and specific scenes in the films, and convincingly argues that the kind of novels that could be "successfully Hitchcockized" were usually the ones that found "a middle way between first-person narration . . . and multiple points of view."

Readers of this anthology will learn a good deal about Hitchcock's source material that critics have seldom considered or simply haven't known. Let me mention a few of the essays from which I learned things and that give a sense of the variety on display: Sidney Gottlieb offers a richly informative study of *The Pleasure Garden* by "Oliver Sandys" (Marguerite Florence Barclay) and the two surviving versions of the Hitchcock film, one from the British Film Institute and the other from the Raymond Rohauer archive; David Sterritt gives us a detailed and intriguing discussion of relatively small but significant changes that Hitchcock and Arthur Laurents made to Patrick Hamilton's *Rope*; Ina Rae Hark reveals the "submerged" connection between *Dial M for Murder* and television drama; Constantine Verevis investigates the reasons for Hitchcock's decision to make a film based largely on the first third of Helen Simpson's *Under Capricorn*; and Pamela Robertson Wojcik, who has recently written a fascinating book on "apartment" films (*The Apartment Plot* [2011]), leads us on a tour through the complicated development of the script for *Rear Window* and the subsequent legal wrangles over the film's "authorship," which ended by favoring the claims of the deceased Cornell Woolrich's literary agent.

One of the more unusual and innovative essays is Mary Hammond's analysis of Hitchcock's silent adaptation of Hall Caine's *The Manxman*. Hammond describes Caine as a "Christian socialist" and a specialist in high Victorian melodrama; I was surprised when she tells us that in the late nineteenth century *The Manxman* was not only more popular than Anthony Hope's *The Prisoner of Zenda* and Rudyard Kipling's *The Jungle Book,* but also in some literary quarters more admired than Thomas Hardy's *Tess of the D'Urbervilles.* The novel appeared first as an illustrated magazine serial and soon after its book publication Caine adapted it for the theater; then in 1916, Caine gave his endorsement to a silent film adaptation by Loane Tucker (now lost). There is no evidence to suggest that Hitchcock saw any of the "paratext" of illustration and stage design surrounding the novel, but Hammond is correct in arguing that studies of adaptation need to give more attention to such matters. As an example of what could be done in this vein, see Guerric DeBona's recent book, *Film Adaptation in the Hollywood Studio Era* (2010), which shows how much Selznick's *David Copperfield* (1934) owed to "the Victorian visual imagination." Even if we can't trace the images of Hitchcock's *The Manxman* to specific visual sources, there is little doubt that the film was influenced at a distance by the visual culture surrounding popular culture in the late Victorian and early modernist period.

Unique among books about adaptation or appropriation, *Hitchcock at the Source* is a model for future work in the area—although I'm not sure any other single film director could provide such an interesting focus. The writers in this volume are admirably unconcerned with the cultural status or fame of the materials that prompted the films; they give priority to cinema over literature, but pay as much close attention to Francis Iles and Ethel Lina White as to John Buchan and Joseph Conrad. (As with the *Companion*, I wish more attention had been paid to the Hitchcock-directed TV shows, which drew on some of the major writers of crime or horror fiction.) Their discussion of the similarities or differences between the films and the sources has primarily to do with what such things tell us about the formation of the director's unquestioned art; and yet one of the side benefits or byproducts of their work is that they give us a sense of the rich loam of popular and sometimes "legitimate" theater and fiction from the late nineteenth and twentieth century out of which Hitchcock's films blossomed.

If I had some idea of where Hitchcock studies will or should go in the future, I might try to go there myself. It's safe to say that the Hitchcock industry will continue for as long as there are academic film studies, and that writings about

Hitchcock will mirror developments in the humanities in general. Hitchcock is unique among filmmakers, not only in the degree of interest he inspires but also in the ability of his films to sustain a critical discourse that responds to every new paradigm; and as long as the academic industry devoted to his work can produce scholarship and criticism as sophisticated as what we find in these anthologies, it will surely be worth reading.

Contributors

Erika Balsom is assistant professor of film studies at Carleton University. She is currently at work on a book manuscript on the moving image in art after 1990.

Charles Barr is Emeritus Professor of Film and TV at the University of East Anglia, and Adjunct Professor in the John Huston School at the National University of Ireland, Galway. His publications include *Ealing Studios*, *English Hitchcock*, and, in the BFI Classics series, *Vertigo*. He is currently working with Alain Kerzoncuf on a collection *Hitchcock: Lost and Found*.

John Hellmann is Professor of English at The Ohio State University, where he is a member of the interdisciplinary Film Studies Faculty. Among his books are *American Myth and the Legacy of Vietnam* and *The Kennedy Obsession: The American Myth of JFK*, both published by Columbia University Press. He is currently working on a book on Hitchcock's films of the late fifties and early sixties.

Gergely Hubai is currently a Ph.D. student in the American Studies Doctoral Program at Eötvös Loránd University, where he is also a deputy lecturer in the Film Department. His main research interests, in addition to Hitchcock, are music in the James Bond films and rejected film scores.

Thomas Leitch teaches English and directs the Film Studies Program at the University of Delaware. His most recent books are *Film Adaptation and Its Discontents: From* Gone with the Wind *to* The Passion of the Christ and *A Companion to Alfred Hitchcock*, coedited with Leland Poague.

James Naremore is Emeritus Chancellors' Professor at Indiana University and a writer-at-large for *Film Quarterly*. His most recent book is *Sweet Smell of Success* (BFI, 2010). Currently he is working on a collection of his essays.

Deborah Thomas is the author of *Beyond Genre: Melodrama, Comedy and Romance in Hollywood Films* and *Reading Hollywood: Spaces and Meanings in American Film*, as well as a monograph on *Buffy the Vampire Slayer* and numerous essays, including several on Hitchcock. Until her retirement, she was Professor of Film Studies at the University of Sunderland in the UK.